It is always goo[...] Christians and [...] how God wen[...] to use them to bring other people to himself. That's what this book is about. God took ordinary men and women, some of whom had faced big problems in their own lives, and saved them. Then he used them as evangelists in the streets of London. Their stories are fascinating, their work is a slog but it's never dull. Light in the City is a good read. As magazine editors say, 'it's full of human interest'.

Maureen McKenna
Founder of the Open Door Trust,
Glasgow

In today's pagan society evangelism must be more than inviting people to attend meetings. We need evangelists to take the gospel to where people are, which is the kind of evangelism in which LCM is engaged. Here we have testimonies which demonstrate the power of Christ to change lives which are being ruined by the depravity of modern inner city life, such as drugs, alcohol addiction and sexual promiscuity. At the same time we are given a realistic selection of examples in that not all of them live happily ever after – life isn't like that. Indeed apparent 'failures' are included, but with the conclusion, 'We keep on praying'. This book should be read by all who have a concern for evangelism which is relevant to the 21st century.

Canon Kenneth Prior

Heart stopping portrayals of daring rescues by the emergency services have become a feature of our TV schedules. In these life and death situations the rescue teams risk their lives to help others. The personal stories in this book put us at the scene of the action where God is saving people from dire situations. In many cases those who have been on the receiving end of such costly kindness have themselves joined God's emergency rescue team as London City Missionaries. His grace truly is amazing."

James McAllen
London City Mission

For Esmé

with love

from Angus and June

LIGHT IN THE CITY

Irene Howat

Christian Focus

All rights reserved. No part of this publication may be reproduced, stored in a retrieval system, or transmitted, in any form, by any means, electronic, mechanical, photocopying, recording or otherwise without the prior permission of the publisher or a license permitting restricted copying. In the U.K. such licenses are issued by the Copyright Licensing Agency, 90 Tottenham Court Road, London W1P 9HE.

ISBN 1-85792-723-0

© Copyright Christian Focus Publications 2002

Published in 2002
by
Christian Focus Publications, Ltd
Geanies House, Fearn, Tain,
Ross-shire, IV20 1TW, U.K.
and
London City Mission, 175 Tower
Bridge Road, LONDON, SE1 2AH

www.christianfocus.com

Cover Design by Alister MacInnes

Printed and bound by
Cox & Wyman, Reading, Berkshire

Contents

Dedication

For John and Nancy

>> *Introduction*

Some people love the buzz of London; they enjoy being part of that huge city's life. For some it is a place to escape to, where they can be anonymous, alone. And for others, the men and women who work as London City Missionaries, it is where they draw near to those they meet, sharing with them the story of how the Lord changed their lives. Through their humble ministry, high-fliers have come to know the Most High God, ordinary men and women have met the man Jesus, and some of those at the bottom of society's heap have met the King of Kings who was himself an outcast and who remembers and understands what that feels like. In *Light in the City*, London City Missionaries tell how they came to faith in Christ Jesus. A number of those who have become Christians through LCM's work also share their stories. But not all who hear about Jesus put their trust in him, and the book reflects that reality. There are many lights in London, but none to compare with the Light of the World, the Lord Jesus Christ.

One >> Neil Kinghorn

I was brought up in a good family. We were happy and we were friends with each other. The family had no church connection at all and we didn't feel any need of it. We were fine as we were. Some children I knew went to Sunday School, but I certainly didn't want to go to school on a Sunday. I didn't actually want to go to school any day of the week. School for me was a struggle and I wasn't really very happy there. I couldn't write or spell very well and got a bit of hassle for that and for being in the remedial class. I'm glad I had a happy home to go back to because school was not much fun. If we were taught Christianity at school I don't think it could have been taught very well because I don't remember it at all.

I looked forward to leaving school and to doing my own thing. The freedom was great. I got a job, enjoyed having money in my pocket and hung around with some old school friends in the evenings at weekends. We were into drinking and spent our time at pubs and night-clubs. My idea of life was to have a job to earn money to spend on my kind of fun. The pub scene was so different from school. I could choose my friends and nobody knew or cared whether I could read or spell or talk ancient Greek for that matter. An old school friend introduced me to drugs. I'd done drinking and knew what it could do for me, but drugs opened a whole new world of experience. Then I hung out with a couple of other friends who took LSD and marijuana. My drinking tailed off as I spent what I earned on drugs. We got more involved with the drug scene and I started dealing a little as I had transport and could collect and distribute fairly easily. LSD made us hallucinate. Marijuana mellowed us out and magic mushrooms were very interesting because they were hallucinogenic. I even used to take the lighter gas. Drinking alcohol was nothing in comparison to drugs, it only made me lose my senses and end up being sick. On LSD, marijuana and magic mushrooms I could drive safely, or so I thought.

Problem lifestyle

Dad and Mum knew much of what I was up to, and they saw me coming home drunk or high on drugs. As I was actually very restrained at home and always polite to them they didn't know the worst of what I was involved in. It was more my lifestyle that was a problem to them. I was rarely home at a reasonable time and when I was at home I was very antisocial and stayed in my own room. My parents were always careful what they said, probably because they didn't want to drive me away from home. There must have been many times when my behaviour was difficult and embarrassing for them, but they coped with it very well.

My friends and I used to meet to take LSD together and then we would hallucinate, and when we took magic mushrooms they made us see the weirdest and strangest things. Certain music goes with certain types of drugs and we listened to Reggae music, mostly to Bob Marley, as we went on our marijuana trips. The words seemed so relevant and meaningful. Songs of slavery and lyrics about corrupt government and poverty began to form my life view. In some of his songs Bob Marley quotes the Bible. Because he became a bit of a role model to us we decided to get Bibles and have a look at them. The combination of hallucinogenic drugs, Reggae music and religion really appealed to us and we decided to go for it and become Rastafarians. We went the whole way – our hair was done in dreadlocks and we wore red, gold and green hats; these three colours are important to Rastafarians. And we stopped taking all drugs apart from marijuana. Rastafarians believe that marijuana is the Tree of Life and that taking it helps to connect us to God. As the Bible talks about the Tree of Life being the tree that brings healing to the nations, they see marijuana as being very important. That was the line we took and we were very committed. My poor parents; they really disliked my natural dreadlocks and unkempt beard, though they never said so. To the rest of the family I was just a misfit.

Our information about Rastafarianism was acquired through videos and books as well as by listening to Reggae music. Rastafarianism was unheard of in our town. My only friends at that time were six others who believed in the things as I did and we all rented bedsits in the same house. As there were no Rasta churches near us we had fellowship together and were very close-knit. We were a little community of seven and happy to stay that way and to have nothing to do with anyone else at a social level.

Rastafarianism

Although much of what we believed seemed to us to be from the Bible I now know how mistaken we were. Rastafarianism grew slowly from the late 1800s as a result of slavery. Marcus Garvey, a leader of the black consciousness movement in the 1920s, prophesied that black people should look to Africa where a black king would be crowned, and that a great day of deliverance would come through him. A few years later, Ras Tafari was crowned King Selassie of Ethiopia. He was immediately hailed as the King of Kings and Lord or Lords by a group of people who took his name and called themselves Rastafarians. Despite Selassie being dead by the time we became Rastas, many believed that he was still alive, that he had ascended to heaven in much the same way as Jesus did, and that he would lead blacks back to their original homeland of Ethiopia.

When people saw my friends and I coming, they crossed the road until they were past us. Nobody liked us. They thought we looked odd and odd means dangerous; and they knew we took drugs. Though we weren't aware of it at the time they even got up a petition to have us moved out of the house we shared. If only they had known it, Rastas actually live a very strict life. They are encouraged not to eat meat and they don't take drugs other than marijuana. They are taught to love humanity and not to be worldly. That's not all. Rastas are meant to stifle jealousy, hatred, gossip, envy and treachery. That should have made us good neighbours!

As we were the only Rastafarians in the area we travelled up to London to meet others and to go to Reggae concerts. But over time we became disillusioned. We were told that Selassie was the son of God, but as we read our Bibles we saw that wasn't true. Even though we were following Rasta teaching some of those we met in London had a bad attitude to us because we were not black. They weren't all like that, but enough of them were that we felt out of it. It also upset us that although they talked and sang about brotherly love, yet there was no warmth in their greeting to us. They were also quick as anything to rip us off over marijuana sales.

We stepped back a bit from Rastafarianism and started asking all kinds of questions of all kinds of people. My brother-in-law found a book that Jehovah's Witnesses had left at his mum's house and we all read it. From our reading of the book it seemed that Jehovah's Witnesses had more answers than anyone else to the questions we were asking about the Bible and about God the Father, Jesus Christ and the Holy Spirit.

A change of direction

Because of that my friends and I went to the local Kingdom Hall but they wouldn't let us in because we were not wearing shirts! They kept us talking outside for over two hours but they wouldn't take us through the door. The following week we went to another Kingdom Hall and just walked right in. The reception there was very different. We were welcomed kindly and courteously. Some Jehovah's Witnesses were willing to come and study with us, but they didn't come back after the first time because we smoked marijuana as we studied. However, they sent an elder and the presiding elder from the meeting to see us. It meant a lot that they were interested enough to do that.

Before long we had swallowed their teaching whole and tried to do all they told us. Overnight we stopped smoking marihuana, every one of us. I didn't find that as difficult as it might sound because the Bible said it was wrong and I was so deeply into studying I hardly missed it. We had our dreadlocks cut off and we threw out our hats. Not only that, but we got suits, shirts and ties and started going round the doors with the Witnesses. For nine months we went to every single meeting that was held and in that time we studied material that was usually covered in two or three years. The Watchtower Society produced all the study material we used and it was fully backed up by well chosen Bible verses. The Jehovah's Witnesses encouraged us to read the Bible, but only their own New World Translation.

Jayne, my girlfriend, and I had been living together all the time we were Rastafarians, but because the Witnesses told us we couldn't do that we got married. When the group of us decided that the Jehovah's Witnesses had got it all together we asked to be baptized, but because they only baptize at large meetings in public stadia we had to wait a while. During that waiting time an evangelist from the local church visited around the area and when he came to our door we asked him in. Jayne and I were there along with five or six JW friends. We suggested to the man that we do a Bible study together because we thought we could convert him, although the fact that he was on the doorstep at all surprised us as we'd been told by JWs that ordinary Christians didn't do evangelism. He came back for a number of studies and really made us think.

An eye-opener

We'd met many people when we were doing visitation who said they were Christians but who had no idea what they believed, and others who flatly contradicted each other; but this man certainly knew his stuff and it seemed to come from the Bible. For weeks we discussed our beliefs with him and he showed us from God's Word where we were wrong. Unlike the Jehovah's Witnesses he only ever used the Bible to back up what he said, never any other source material. I didn't give the evangelist a hard time but I was extremely thorough, needing a great deal of biblical confirmation before I would concede a point. The evangelist, who spoke with authority, was very capable of explaining the differences between the teaching of the Jehovah's Witness and the teaching of the Word of God. At the end of it all my brother-in-law and I realized that what he was telling us was true.

But we had a problem. We had been Rastafarians and had discovered what they taught was wrong, and we'd been Jehovah's Witnesses till we found out that what they taught was wrong. We didn't want to go to the evangelist's church then discover six months down the line that it was wrong too. My brother-in-law and I prayed about it and talked about it for hours. We had plenty of opportunity to do that because we worked together as window cleaners and we lived in the same house. One night, after reading the Bible, God really spoke to my heart, telling me that it was not by my works that I could be saved but by what Jesus had done for me. The Lord removed the scales from my eyes and I saw for the first time that it was he, not all my hard work, who could save me. I started going to the evangelist's church and within a very short time I was out on the streets knocking the doors with him and telling people that they could only be saved through the Lord Jesus Christ.

Although I tried to reason with Jayne, she continued to attend the Kingdom Hall.

Compared with the service at the Kingdom Hall, which was very tightly controlled the church seemed so easy-going. Jehovah's Witnesses sing only to set tapes, there is no free prayer or worship, and each Sunday the same study is followed in all Kingdom Halls worldwide. Jayne did come to church with me sometimes, but she found the relaxed atmosphere and people clapping during the singing made her feel very uncomfortable whereas I enjoyed the freedom and the unconditional warmth and friendship so much. It was such a relief to know that my salvation didn't depend on attendance at services or on how much evangelistic activity I took part in. Jehovah's Witnesses have to keep a record of their door-to-door work to prove that they are still active, and they believe that failing to keep up their evangelistic activity puts at risk their future hope of living on paradise earth. Although Jayne was told by the JWs to try to persuade me back into the Kingdom Hall, she did not attempt to do that because she herself was not sure who was right and who was wrong. A few nights after the birth of our first child, while asleep in hospital, the

Lord spoke to Jayne in a dream and she came to saving faith in him.

Looking back

Initially my parents didn't understand about our conversion but they were quietly pleased about it as they thought it would make us more normal. I'm sad when I think of the grief I've caused them over the years. Dad and Mum didn't like it at all when we were Rastafarians, but they were subdued in their objections. They must have been so embarrassed sometimes as we were the only ones with dreadlocks in the town and our lifestyle was very different from everyone else. Then when we became Jehovah's Witnesses they were so concerned they asked us to stay Rastas because JWs weren't allowed to have a blood transfusion regardless of how much they needed it. And birthdays and Christmas hurt them too because JWs don't celebrate things like that. Because we were such a close-knit family that was a really big thing. So although as a JW I cut off my dreadlocks and wore a smart suit and tie, the fact that I was a Witness at all caused my parents a lot of sadness and concern.

Looking back over the ten years since

then I can see how God has worked in my life, using every experience, even the bad ones. As Rastafarians we would never have entertained going to a white church, even though we were white, because of the issue of slavery. He used that time to help me work through all sorts of racial issues despite the fact we lived on the South Coast where there were no ethnic groups. Then God used the Jehovah's Witnesses to get us out of Rastafarianism, before sending the Christian evangelist to show us the wrong road we had taken. But I owe a lot to the JWs. When I left school my reading skills were not very good at all and the Watchtower Society's method of study helped to improve them. The whole group took part, reading round and each reading a part. As someone who had always been laughed at and teased at school because I couldn't read, that was a big thing. At first I was scared stiff, but it had to be done. Reading in front of others and working my way through the JW study programme helped my reading a lot. Although it was very difficult at first, I developed a real keenness for reading and became convinced of the power of the written word.

Broken barriers

Having discovered the truth, I was very enthusiastic to tell other people and I went round the doors with the good news. Our evangelist friend had done a year with the London City Mission some time before that and he told me about the work he did then. It sounded just what I wanted to do but didn't have the time to do because I was working full time. Jayne and I decided to apply to the Mission, but after filling up the application form all sorts of barriers were raised. We couldn't afford to give up work. Our fellow church members couldn't commit themselves to support us financially. Where would we live? The interview sorted these things out. We discovered missionaries were paid a wage and provided with a house. The day of the interview God broke all the barriers down.

My first impressions of the London City Mission were very encouraging. The Mission staff and headquarters team were really helpful, especially during my four month long training period. We had two children then, Joshua and Hannah. Jayne and the children stayed on the South Coast while I did my training, and our third child, Bethany, was born at that time. The Mission was very good, allowing me to go back home at weekends. The chap I was training with said I only needed to be back for the Sunday afternoon meeting which gave me as long as possible with Jayne and the children. That sort of kindness meant a great deal to us. Things were so different from what we thought they would be. We had worried about where we would live and what we would live on. God says that he will provide for all our needs and that is what he did through the Mission. For me that was a new experience of God's faithfulness. There were other blessings too, the high standard of Bible teaching and lectures among them.

Having completed my training, we were placed in Downham, based in a Christian Centre in the middle of a big council estate. One of the main parts of my work over the six years we were there was visiting door-to-door. That's the kind of work the Lord has really put into my heart. I feel I've been given such good news that Jesus is my Saviour that I've just got to go out and tell other people. My own experience shows me that the best way of doing that is to knock on folk's doors. It was because the evangelist knocked on our door and was prepared to come back over and over again to our home to answer our questions from the Bible patiently that we came to know the Lord. That's the work I most want to do.

God has given us some real blessings. I met Paul and Chris during door-to-door visiting. They allowed me to do a regular Bible study with them and after many months Paul became a Christian. Some time later Chris, who had previously attended a spiritualist church, also put her faith in Jesus. Iris, who came from a Catholic background, was always willing to talk about life. Eventually she came along to the Centre and after a couple of years she gave her heart to the Lord. Seeing people coming to know the Lord and growing in the knowledge of Jesus is what makes it all worthwhile. We still do door-to-door work in our present placement in Dagenham. Our days are very busy with the mother and toddlers' group, clubs for small children, older youngsters and teenagers, a Bible study meeting, prayer meeting and Sunday service and Sunday School. Because we have such a full programme there is not enough time to do as much door-to-door visiting as I would like – but that's because I'd do it all day every day if I could!

Two >> Harry Vallance

My first meeting with John was when he was working in the offices of the Great Western Railway and I was the London City Missionary to the railways. It was his manager who approached me and asked me to speak to him. John was an alcoholic and his boss was concerned that he might lose his job because of his drink problem. He also suffered from depression. I spoke to John a couple of times in his workplace but the proximity of other workers meant he felt unable to talk about anything of a personal nature. 'Would it be helpful if I visited you at home?' I asked, during one of our conversations. He agreed readily and we set a date for the following week. When the day came I was welcomed into his home and we sat down together with cups of coffee. Instead of talking with me, John put on a record of Wagner's music and for an hour we listened to it together. My immediate reaction to his choice of music was that it would encourage his state of depression rather than help; it was so powerful.

After an hour of listening to Wagner and not speaking at all, John turned the music off. 'That's not what you really came for,' he said, sitting down again. 'What do you want?' We talked together over some of his problems then I read the Scriptures to him, prayed and left. For about three months my visits to his home continued and I saw him in the GWR office too. Although my wife and I had an open house I didn't often invite men I'd met in the railway work back home, but I did ask John and we prayed for him as we waited for his knock at the door.

John's story
When John arrived, later than we'd expected him, he was very, very drunk. I put on some Christian music as he drank the strong coffee my wife made for him. There was no point in talking to my friend that day because he was in a terrible state. Instead we allowed him time to be calm and quiet then we had a prayer and a Bible reading before I gave him a run home. It was some days later that John told me his story. 'I

reckon you saved my life,' he began. 'The day I arranged to come and see you I heard that my divorce had been finalized and all I wanted to do was take my life. The only thing that stopped me was that you had invited me to your home. That's why I was so drunk. When I left work I went into the first pub I came to and had a double scotch, and I went in to every one I passed on my way to your house and had another.'

John and I continued to see each other and I made a special point of visiting him at Christmas, thinking he might be lonely because I knew he was on his own. During that visit we talked about the Lord and of his need for a Saviour. Before I left, John and I knelt side by side before a little table in his living room and he asked for the Lord's forgiveness and cleansing. I believe that night he was saved. My friend began to attend the Christian Union we held at Paddington and he bought himself a Bible and started to read it. I remember one day watching John on the platform as he walked towards me. He was smiling. 'You're going to get into trouble if you're not careful,' I teased. 'What do you mean?' John asked. I laughed, 'I've just seen your teeth for the first time.' Since he came to faith even his face had changed. He had lost his pathos and was wearing a smile.

By reading his Bible and attending Christian Union John continued to grow in his faith. I don't think he ever went to any church, just the CU meetings. Four years after his conversion he retired and went to live by the seaside. For some that would have been delightful after a life spent working in the city, but for John it was not. He found retirement and all the changes that came along with it very difficult and I think his depression became a problem again.

One day a letter arrived from his aunt, telling me that John had committed suicide. I visited her and attended his funeral. After the burial I went back to John's flat with his aunt. 'Is there anything of his you'd like?' she asked. There in the room was the very table my friend had knelt beside when he asked the Lord to save him. I told his aunt the story and said I'd very much like that little table. I still have it, and it reminds me of a friend of whom I have bitter-sweet memories, but who I hope to see once again in glory.

Brian

A London City Missionary did regular
door-to-door visiting in the block of flats in
which Brian lived. As his door was never
answered, the missionary assumed that the
tenant was out at work. It was only when a
neighbour told him about Brian's situation
that he discovered otherwise. On his next
few visits to the flats the missionary knocked
at Brian's door on the way up the stairs,
giving him ample time to answer, and did
the same on the way down; both times with
no response. But one day the two met.
Brian, elderly and agitated, was just coming
out of his door as the other man reached it.
The missionary introduced himself and
asked if there was anything he could do to
help. Instinctively Brian shook his head and
said no, but the missionary noticed the old
man was holding a prescription and he
offered to go to the chemist for him. Brian
stood for a minute, unsure of what to do,
then accepted the offer.

On his return the missionary knocked
at the door, and when there was no reply he
knocked again then let himself in. Brian
and his wife Molly lived in the small flat.
They were both in their late seventies and
had no children. Molly suffered from

Alzheimer's and was confused and jittery, especially if Brian was out of sight. She had turned night into day, keeping her husband awake most of the night then sleeping off and on all day. The only time Molly slept soundly enough that Brian felt able to leave her was first thing in the morning. He did his shopping then, at the corner shop that opened at 6 a.m. In a very real way they were both imprisoned by Molly's condition.

Confused and cut off

Neighbours had offered help but the poor woman was suspicious of strangers, and because her short-term memory was so badly affected, everyone was a stranger to her except Brian. And she didn't even recognize him for who he was. Sometimes she called him by her late brother's name; sometimes she called him Dad, and sometimes even Doctor. As strangers upset Molly, Brian steered clear of offers of help, both from neighbours and from the social services. Although the flat was a bit of a muddle, it was obvious that Brian did his very best to look after his wife and to keep their home. To the missionary it was more than obvious that the elderly man was utterly exhausted and stressed to the limit.

Brian explained that this was a bad patch because his wife had a chest infection, but as the two men talked while Molly slept, it became clear that life for Brian had been one long bad patch for the past eight or nine years, and that this was really only a very little bit worse than usual.

Brian's big fear was that he would die before his wife and that she would be 'put into a home'. The missionary offered to help in any way he could, adding that his wife would also be willing to assist. That was the start of weekly visits. Over the following months the young couple visited and shopped, and the missionary's wife sat with Molly to let Brian out for a short time. At first they only did this while she was asleep, but eventually he was prepared to leave her awake. This was greatly helped by the fact that Molly seemed to think that the missionary's wife was Lucy, a girl she had played with as a child.

Calm in the storm

As the elderly lady's condition deteriorated and she became even more muddled, she began to be less agitated. Her sense of knowing she was confused gradually left her, and she became more tranquil.

Although this made life easier for Brian he found two things very hard: that his wife now had no clue who he was, and that she lost her inhibitions, and some things she said and did embarrassed him. For years Molly was from time to time unsure who Brian was; now he began to understand how she felt. He was not in the least confused, but the woman he cared for bore almost no resemblance to his wife. Although Molly was still alive, Brian felt as if she had died. The missionary and his wife committed themselves to seeing the couple through this terrible time. Brian was deeply appreciative of what they did, and Molly giggled like a girl when her friend 'Lucy' came to see her. Brian even allowed the missionary to read a few verses from the Bible and pray before the end of each visit. 'I'll come to the Centre one day,' he often said, 'but I can't leave the wife just now.'

For over two years the missionary couple supported Brian and Molly. Being able to get out did Brian good and he coped better with his situation. As Molly was more tranquil, neighbours were able to help without upsetting her. The lady next door who had originally told the missionary about Brian cooked the couple a meal twice or three times a week. What especially encouraged the missionary was that Brian seemed to look forward to the Bible reading and prayer, and he brought up the subject of Christianity quite often, mostly related to the fact that he longed to be sure that Molly would be at peace when she died. He accepted Christian literature and talked it over during visits. And he began to read the Bible. The first the young couple knew of this was when during one visit Molly asked her husband to read her a story about Jesus. Brian took a Bible from the drawer and read to his wife the story of Jesus calming a storm. 'She never gets tired of that story,' he said, closing the Bible.

Why?
Brian woke up one morning to find that his wife had died in her sleep. He rushed to his next-door neighbour who called the doctor and then ran to see if she could do anything. Discovering Molly was beyond help, she went home and phoned the missionary. Brian asked him to take Molly's funeral and that was what happened. The young missionary couple continued to support Brian over his time of bereavement. At first the old man was just full of gratitude that

he had been able to keep his wife at home till she died. But some months after Molly's death Brian began to question why she should have had Alzheimer's, why he was left on his own, why they were unable to have children. The missionary invited Brian to the Christian Centre now that he was free to come, but then he was unwilling to leave the house. It was as though he felt safe there. His neighbour continued to care for him, and the missionary couple tried to as well. But Brian drew back from their friendship. His welcome grew less warm and he seemed to lose interest in the Bible reading and prayer. There were no more discussions on Christian things and no suggestion that one day he'd come to a service. The missionary and his wife still visit, and they will continue to do so as long as Brian opens the door to them. But they have a feeling that one day when they knock there will be no reply. Brian has a spyhole in his door and he might decide not to answer when he sees who is there.

London City Missionaries befriend young and old alike, caring for them for their own sakes while hoping and praying that they will meet the best friend of all, the Lord Jesus Christ.

Richard

Right from his childhood Richard heard about Jesus. He came from a poor area in North London and had often seen London City Mission in action. His father was a drunk and his mother struggled to keep the family of four together. Many times there was no food on the table. A missionary working in a nearby Christian Centre, made aware of the family's situation by a neighbour, went with his wife to see if they could be of any help. On the day they arrived, Richard's mother was at her wit's end. There was neither food for their next meal nor any heating in the flat. The woman was only too glad to accept the offer of a meal at the Centre and, while the children were being entertained in another room, she poured out her whole story.

Her partner (they were not married) was the father of only three of the children. Richard, the second eldest and the only boy, was not his. He had been born while her partner was spending a lengthy period in prison. As a result of this the boy had an especially hard time and when the man he called Dad came in drunk, it was Richard he lashed out at. The missionary had seen the child out on the streets at all hours and realized now why this was so. As her story poured out it became clear that there were times when she feared for Richard's safety. She had considered approaching the social services, but was afraid that she would lose her boy and not see him again. It was clear that she loved the lad and was very willing that the missionary should do what he could to help.

A place of refuge

A pattern was established over the years that followed. The man's drinking habits were predictable in that he drank when he had money and didn't when he had none. He was a labourer who did work on a jobbing basis. At the end of weeks in which he worked Richard stayed with the missionary and his wife and when his dad was sober again he went home. Prior to this arrangement the boy's school work had been neglected and his behaviour disruptive but as the months passed he calmed down and his teachers began to realize that he was brighter than they had thought. This was helped by the missionary's wife, a former teacher, who tutored the boy when he stayed with them and made herself available to help with his homework at other times too.

There were children's meetings at the Centre, and Richard and his brother and sisters attended them, at first only because the place was warm and they were given juice and biscuits, but through time they became integrated into the clubs and seemed to enjoy them. Richard was, however, the only one who showed a real interest in the spiritual side of the club, and as a young teenager he often asked the missionary's wife questions about what had been discussed. She never pressed the lad into committing himself to the Lord, but she did point him to Jesus when the opportunity arose and there seemed to be a spark in Richard's heart. He accepted Bible reading notes, saying he would use them with the Gideon New Testament he had been given at school. Occasional comments the boy made encouraged the missionary as they indicated that the lad was reading God's Word.

When he was fourteen his father's drinking became such a problem that he was unable to get work. For a while this meant that he was less of a problem at home, but the craving for alcohol got the better of him and he broke into licensed premises intending to steal enough to keep him going for a while. Unfortunately the owner of the shop was still in the building when he broke in and in the fight that followed the man was badly injured. Richard's dad was charged with a serious assault, as well as breaking and entering, and he found himself in prison again. The boy felt a responsibility for his family and looked for part-time work. When he told the missionary what his job was the man's heart sank. Richard had found employment delivering goods from a shop which the missionary was certain was being used for peddling drugs.

Downward spiral

Because he was working the lad was unable to attend the club for teenagers, nor was he free to seek help with his homework. As a result his grades at school slipped and he began to lose the self-respect that his teachers and others had worked hard to build up. When the missionary hadn't seen the boy for several weeks he felt concerned enough to visit his home. It was much improved from the first time he had been there. Now money coming in was spent on the family rather than on drink and it was altogether a happier place, but news of Richard was not so good. It seemed that he was working long hours and his mother had had a visit from his guidance teacher at school enquiring about an unlikely number of absences.

Now very concerned, the man made a point of finding Richard and inviting him to his home for a meal. There was nothing unusual in that invitation as the lad had often eaten with the family. But Richard's reaction was more than unusual, he told the man who had cared for him never to speak to him again, and certainly not in public. He said that he was no longer a boy and that he was done with the Mission. And that was the last time they spoke. The missionary couple continued to pray for Richard even though the only news they had of him was bad. Before long he was known as a drug addict, then he was arrested for pushing drugs outside a school. When the missionary tried to visit him in prison, the young man would not see him. But the couple that cared for him over several years still pray for him knowing that God is able to save him even from the mess he is in now.

Three >> Jamie Stewart

I was brought up in a travelling family in the remote north west of Scotland. In some parts of the country we would have been known as tinkers. Though my parents didn't travel, my grandparents on both sides had. Being from a travelling family had quite an impact on our lives as children. We were different and we knew it. And we felt different, even the way we thought didn't seem to be the same as other boys. The Stewarts were travellers and that was just a fact of life. I suppose a family of eight, four boys and four girls, made us different too. There weren't too many families that size in Plockton.

We didn't go to church at all, yet I always believed there was a God. Though I didn't like school, I really did like it when one of my teachers told us stories from the Bible. I can't remember much that I was taught at primary school, or secondary for that matter, but I never forgot one or two Bible stories. My parents were God-fearers, though they were not Christians. Even though my father had a drink problem, he told us off strongly if we misused the Lord's name, and we did sometimes use God's name as a swearword. I remember my parents often speaking about the Lord being over our lives.

I suppose the best way to describe school for me is by saying it was a lonely experience because I didn't fit in. I wasn't good at anything. Teachers and other pupils picked on me and when it got too much for me I just took time off, lots of time. Of course that meant I fell still further behind, was picked on more and grew even more unhappy and defiant. People who knew me probably thought I was fairly outgoing, but that was just a front, a kind of defence; I was actually really quite screwed up inside. Drunkenness was something I knew about because my father had a strong drink problem in those days. I was about eleven when I started smoking and drinking, and I was drunk, very drunk, for the first time when I was twelve. And things didn't get better. I used to drink and smoke with other boys in the village and when my father was drinking I'd help myself to some of his. My parents knew I smoked though I never did in front of my father.

Digging myself into a hole

When I left school I went to work in the local fish factory, but a lot of drinking went on there and I just got deeper and deeper into the lifestyle that went with it and I got involved in drugs a bit too. People think that beautiful areas of Scotland are happy and healthy places to live, but all the problems you find in the city can be found in the country too. Even in Plockton there was something of a drug culture. I sometimes used cannabis, which I got from others lads in the village. I never bought it myself. By the time I was eighteen I was aware of being trapped in a hard drinking, drug taking and sexually immoral life, if you could call it a life. I thought things couldn't get any worse. They did.

I spent a lot of money on a car but I didn't have it for long before I crashed it. It was my fault too. I'd been working night shift the night before in the fish factory and after work I went home to Plockton to get cleaned up, then back into Kyle where I spent the afternoon in the pub drinking. When I left there I headed for another pub some distance away but only got about a mile down the road before I fell asleep for a second at the wheel. The car span out of control and, before I could do anything, it ended up on its side with the driver's door on the ground. Thankfully I wasn't hurt and nobody else was involved. When I pulled myself together I climbed out through the passenger door. But I was in trouble with the police big time and banned from driving. Dad and Mum were sorry for me, I remember that, especially as I'd lost both my licence and car. They thought I'd blown it, and I thought so too. I was in the pits, but there was more and worse to come.

From bad to worse

In October 1989, when I was eighteen, Mum went in to hospital and it was found that she was suffering from breast cancer. She had treatment for it, but at the beginning of the following year her health deteriorated. Words can't begin to describe what it was like then. I knew Mum was dying and I knew I'd messed up my own life. Serious thoughts of suicide went through my head. I planned what I would do. I'd drink myself stupid then go somewhere quiet, there were plenty of places like that around Plockton, and I'd take a pile of pills, fall asleep, and that would be it. Kaput. The end. But even then I knew that wasn't how things were. Somehow I knew for definite that there was a God. I even tried to pray, but in a superstitious way not really believing he could and would answer. Then, on a terrible Sunday in March 1990, Mum died. My life was so messed up that I really didn't grieve; I couldn't. At that point I knew for sure that there was a heaven and a hell, and that I was going to hell.

Somewhere in the midst of my despair I knew that God existed and that he loved me. I *knew* that. Many times I promised him that I was going to go to church to find out about him. But I didn't do it – travelling people don't go to church and I didn't even think I'd be welcome if I did – as a result I fell back into the cycle of drinking, depression, taking anti-depressants, seeing the psychiatrist … and so it went on. Of course, every time I went on the drink again after a time off it, things were worse than ever. One night that's just what happened.

I'd been off the bottle for a while and that night I got drunk and was so unutterably upset and hopeless that I broke a beer glass and slashed my arm with it. It wasn't an attempted suicide, just sheer anger, frustration and loneliness at being whom and what I was. I just couldn't forgive myself.

A lifeline

Months after Mum died I went into Craig Dunnain, a psychiatric hospital in Inverness about eighty miles away from home. I was in a state of deep depression, brought on, I think, by the fact I knew hell was real and I thought I was lost and damned. I tried to talk to the family about it but that didn't work. Roddie Rankin, the Free Church minister in Kyle came to see me when he was doing hospital visiting in Inverness. He wasn't my minister, I didn't have one, but he had visited our home from time to time since Mum died. His visit was just before I was due to go home for a weekend. 'How are you getting home to Plockton?' he asked. I hadn't thought about it. 'I'll give you a lift.' I accepted his offer, and I knew in my heart that this was the point in my life when I had to ask the questions that were torturing me. I might never have another chance.

'When's your church service?' I asked Roddie, as we headed back to Plockton. 'On Sunday at 12.15,' he told me. But he didn't pressure me to go to church. 'Jamie,' he said, 'it doesn't matter what you've done, Jesus can forgive all your sins.' 'The devil will try to take you further away from God,' he told me a little while later. 'The devil is always trying to take me away from God,' I thought. Before he left me that day, Roddie gave me a Christian book to read. As I read it, pictures of hell tortured me once again. 'Will you come to church with me?' I asked one of my brothers. 'OK,' he agreed. 'We'll go next week.' I really hung on to that promise as I set off for another week in hospital. Although I still felt lonely and lost, somehow I knew things were going to be different.

We didn't go to church the following weekend, but when I met Roddie in the village he didn't row me or nag me. He was always so encouraging. One Sunday, not long afterwards, I was in the kitchen having a cup of tea when I had a thought so vivid that it was like actually hearing things. It was as though I could hear people laughing at me for going to church, then in my mind I heard people laughing at Jesus. Suddenly I knew that if that's what they did to him it didn't matter in the least if they laughed at me. Downing my tea, I set out for church, and arrived early. I received such a warm welcome that I knew everyone was pleased to see me. That was a strange feeling and it meant such a lot. Roddie was preaching on 1 Kings 18, and when he spoke I knew that this was God's Word. It was alive! I was overwhelmed. 'Wow!' I thought, 'I'm here. This is it!' As the service went on I felt a peace flow through me. Without using any words I asked God to forgive me my sins.

An insider!

As I walked home one of the church elders passed in his car and beeped his horn and waved. He waved at me, Jamie Stewart! Men like him didn't do things like that. They didn't beep their car horns and wave to the likes of me! Travelling people were on the outside. I was born on the outside. I'd lived on the outside. And this man, and the other people at church, had welcomed me in.

That night I could hardly keep my eyes open, and when I went to bed I slept. These are just simple words, but after what I'd gone through a night's sleep was out of this world. For months and months I'd been afraid to fall asleep in case I went to hell. What was most wonderful of all was the sure and certain knowledge that Jesus is alive. Not that Jesus **was** alive, but that he is, now, really truly alive! That great day of discovery was in February 1991.

I was twenty years old and life had just begun. That summer was wonderful. There was a Billy Graham crusade held in Scotland and the meetings were beamed up to the Isle of Skye, across a narrow strip of sea from Kyle. I went every night and I realized that this was what it was all about. What Billy Graham was preaching about was what had happened to me. Roddie Rankin continued to be a great help and encouragement; I owe him so much for what he did for me then and since. The following February I asked to be taken into church membership. How that happens in the Free Church of Scotland is that applicants are interviewed by the Kirk Session (that's all the elders and the minister) and questioned to make sure their faith is real. I could never have believed that I would have been able to meet with men like that or to talk to them about what was in my heart. I certainly would never have believed that they would have wanted to listen, that they would have wanted to hear me, Jamie Stewart. Plockton is a small place, and they knew very well what I'd been like before and they knew my travelling background. Yet despite all that they listened to my testimony and accepted me as a member. I'd never felt so at home as I did in that small highland congregation.

Over those months I could have been very much on my own; I certainly didn't fit in with my old friends and it might have taken me a while to fit into the church. But it wasn't like that. Roddie spent a lot of time with me, teaching me the basic things that I'd no idea about, not just from the Bible but also about living. And an older couple more or less adopted me into their family. The husband worked with the Blythswood Tract Society, a Christian literature and aid organization, and my involvement with them widened my vision of Christian service. Being in their home was beautiful because I was loved and cared for there. They were like parents to me then and they still are now. One of the things that encouraged me most was that I saw my prayers being answered. God seemed to be interested even in little things, and when I prayed I used to look for his answers. It's so easy to pray and leave it there, not really being interested in what God does with our prayers. But it wasn't like that. I discovered that God really did hear even Jamie Stewart's prayers and that he really did answer them. That was something else!

Beginning to understand

Reading the Bible was more of a struggle. Roddie suggested I start in the gospels and then he guided me to other passages. Of course I delved into other bits and sometimes I felt swamped because I was so ignorant. For example, once I read in the New Testament that the Scriptures were fulfilled and I wished I had the Scriptures to see how they had been fulfilled. I didn't realize that the Scriptures in that context were the books of the Old Testament and that I was holding them in my hand! It took some time for me to discover that the Old Testament was also about Jesus. God knew what I needed and he led me to a retired missionary who lived in Plockton. He spent some time with me and helped to sort me out. It was through him that I discovered that the Old Testament was about Jesus, through a chapter in Isaiah that is all about the Lord's death. There is almost as much detail in that chapter, which was written more than six hundred years before the crucifixion, as there is in the New Testament. To me that was just amazing!

I became deeply involved in the work of the congregation, going to all the services and prayer meetings and anything else that was going on. And I also volunteered to help locally with Blythswood, which meant assisting in the distribution of Christian literature and in the collection and distribution of aid, mostly to Eastern Europe. Very soon I realized that there was more to Christianity than I had thought. My vision was becoming worldwide. Quite often we had Walter Jackson, who worked with Muslims in Africa, speaking in church, and every time I heard him my heart was challenged. Listening to him was like reading a fascinating book and what he said really challenged me. As he shared his experience, telling us about the people he had met, the risks he had taken and God's care and protection over him, I was deeply challenged to take the gospel to Muslim people.

All change

My cousin Donald was converted in 1993. He had read some awful thing a man wrote about the world coming to an end that very year and he was filled with a terrible fear that he was going to hell. He came to my house and asked where Roddie lived, then headed off in the direction of the manse. Some time later that evening, when he came back having had a long talk about things with the minister, I gave him a Billy Graham booklet that finished with a prayer. When he went home, Donald prayed that prayer and was converted. Although we were cousins we had never been close, we just said 'hello' to each other in the pub. That all changed when he became a Christian. There were so few young converted people in the area that Donald and I were really grateful for each other. It was a wonderful honeymoon period for both of us. Donald worked in the fish factory and I was by then a fisherman. Every night we met for fellowship and prayer. Sometimes we read together all night, other times we spent the whole night praying and we watched a lot of Christian videos too.

In July that same year there was a congregational fellowship meeting after our communion service. The visiting preacher gave his testimony, part of which was about time he had spent on the *Logos*, a mission ship run by Operation Mobilisation which travels around the world visiting different ports and being involved in mission in each one. As I had known for about six months that the Lord was calling me to do some kind of mission, what I heard that night really spoke to my heart. I applied to Operation Mobilisation and was accepted as a member of a team that was to run a summer campaign in Belgium. I don't know what good I did there, but it certainly did me a lot of good. Then I was accepted for the *Logos*. That was a gift, but it was really hard work too. We all did forty hours of practical work on board each week as well as being involved in mission. For me the great thing about that experience was meeting Christians from all over the world and learning to have fellowship with them. It was a wonderful demonstration of what it means to be brothers and sisters in Christ. I'd not thought of it before, but because we have the same Heavenly Father we really are brothers and sisters.

Terrified!
We worked a lot with people and sometimes
I met folk who were just as I had been. I
felt as though I could see into their lives and
I knew there was hope for them, even if
others did not. I knew what God could do
because he had done it for me. Yet there
was once when I was nearly overwhelmed.
The leader of a *Logos* evangelistic team
asked me to go with him to visit a prison on
the island of St Vincent. I was terrified! We
met with about forty men in an open
courtyard. The smell was awful; it was a
terrible place. But God helped me to keep
smiling and there was a real sense of the
Lord's power during the meeting. There
were a couple of men there who had been
converted in prison, but the others weren't
Christians. One of the believing prisoners
came to the front and sang a song about
Jesus that began, 'Because he lives I can face
tomorrow.' It was so moving to hear those
beautiful words in that awful place and to
know that even there that prisoner knew the
words were true. One of the other prisoners
ran forward to me after the service and asked
if he could have my Bible. He was so
desperate for God's Word. That was such a
precious moment.

After the service the team went to see men on death row. They were dressed in white shorts and tee shirts and had only a small mattress and a Bible in their cells. One of them had murdered his girlfriend and her two children. He was so terrified of what was going to happen to him that he was on medication to help him cope with the fear. 'They've condemned me,' he told me urgently. 'Do you know what that means?' I said I did, but I went on to explain that sin had already condemned him as it has condemned all of us, and that God is able to forgive us our sins. I showed him in the Bible that Jesus says whoever believes on him will have eternal life. I don't know if what I said to that poor man penetrated his terror, but I know God is able to do even that.

Monika

While I was on the *Logos* I met another Operation Mobilisation team member and we fell in love. Monika is Swiss and our relationship moved slowly as there were strict rules about these things on the ship. If there hadn't been rules all sorts of problems might have arisen. My time with OM finished in February 1997 and Monika still had some months to go. We were married that October and settled in Switzerland for a time. All the time I was looking to see what the Lord was going to open up for us.

By then, and through God's wonderful grace, my brother Willie was also a Christian. He was converted while I was on the *Logos* and he had been accepted as a London City Missionary. Monika and I were at his commissioning service and we decided to find out more about LCM ourselves. God had already called my cousin Donald into the same work. Wonderfully LCM accepted us and we are working with them still. The training the Mission gives is very good but I don't think that any training can ever really prepare you for the different situations you come across as a city missionary and for the brokenness of people's lives. Much of our work is door-to-door visiting. One house can be wealthy looking and the one right next door might have no carpets on the floor. So many people we meet seem to be wearing a mask to cover their real selves, but that often begins to slip the better we get to know them. I think that telling people a bit about my background helps those who feel hopeless to realize that there is hope for them. I don't hold myself up as an example, but I do stand alongside people and tell them that I was once a drunk and I took drugs too. There is no reason for me to hold myself up, any difference for the good in my life is all down to Jesus.

When I meet outsiders, I know what it is like to be in their shoes. I know there is hope for them even if they don't feel it. But helping people to realize that and to reach out for God's forgiveness and help is not easy. The congregation in Plockton made me feel loved and that spoke to me more than words. That's what I try to do with the outsiders I get to know through my work. I try to show them that they are special to me and even more special to God. Monika and I have two small sons, David and Elias, and she is also involved with the Mission, especially the mothers' and toddlers' club and in the children's ministry. It's a privilege to serve the Lord together and to pray together for the people we meet.

Thorny roses

The Christian life is great but it's not a bed of roses, or if it is there are plenty of thorns on the roses. People I was really close to before I became a believer sometimes attacked my faith and that was hard. It still is. Then there are the struggles against sin that will go on as long as I'm in this world. Some problem areas have been dealt with. Drink was one of them. The last time I had a desire to drink was at a wedding in 1991 and it affected me very deeply. I went home that night and really had it out with God. Thankfully that has never happened again. It was a year after my conversion before I was able to give up smoking and there are many things left in my life still to be faced. The problem of sin will be there till the day I die, but not for a second after that. When things are tough that's a great comfort, but still being a sinner, even a converted one, ensures life is never too comfortable!

Four >> Paul James-Griffiths

As it came near Hallowe'en one year I felt I should write a suitable leaflet to put through the doors around the church where I was working as an evangelist. On the Sunday after they were delivered, four young women, who had been involved in witchcraft, turned up at church in response to the leaflets. They had thrown away their witchcraft gear and wanted to know about Jesus. I was on holiday that week but, when I got back to work, I went to visit them. Two of them were especially keen: Tammy, who came from a Jewish background, and Kelly, an Australian. These young women had been searching for spiritual enlightenment, and were dabbling in all sorts of different religions and New Age thinking. They accepted that Jesus was a historical person but viewed him as some sort of New Age guru. When we discussed Christ, it became clear that they thought that everyone had some good in them, that the good was Christ, and that the nearest anyone could get to a god was to use a variety of techniques to realize their own good, the god within. Tammy and Kelly believed that by using various techniques of meditation and occult they could realize 'the god within'.

We began to study the Bible together. Tammy had real problems with the Bible, especially with the concept of the three-in-one God, the Father, Son and Holy Spirit. She viewed Christ as a teacher but could not accept that he was the Messiah, the One promised by God who would redeem his people from their sins. Her Jewish background really coloured her thinking. Kelly was much more open and eventually she prayed for forgiveness and accepted the Lord as her Saviour. But Tammy was struggling. The more she fought against the idea of Jesus as Saviour, the more it troubled her. Even her sleep was disturbed. She suffered from terrible nightmares, seeing row upon row of graves of Jewish people who had been killed in the holocaust. Tammy felt that to accept Jesus was to be a traitor to those who had died for the religion in which she had been brought up. As we continued our Bible studies together the young woman's thinking got into an ever more complicated knot. She could see that Christ had made a real difference to Kelly's life, yet everything in her was rebelling at the thought of Jesus. However, she could only hold out against God's love for so long, and eventually she too became a Christian. That was a moment of great freedom for Tammy and of incredible joy for me! It is especially precious to see a Jewish person embrace her own Messiah.

At home in the squat

I continued to visit the young women in their squat. Their circumstances were dire. The building was very derelict to the extent that the internal walls were falling down. There was no heating at all other than a fire in the middle of one of the rooms, and that was their only cooking facility. They had rigged up some old blankets to keep the worst of the wind off themselves. As soon as Kelly and Tammy became Christians they faced their first big challenge because the group held to a New Age mindset. But the Lord saw the pair of them through that and through many other challenges too. Not only so, but some of the other women also became Christians. When I encouraged them to attend church, sadly their enthusiasm rather put some people off, thus making them feel unwelcome. However, their hearts were right with the Lord and eventually they found a church that recognized the work of grace God had done in them. Before long Tammy and Kelly were leading others to the Lord and they are still doing that today.

Sometimes I feel great frustration because I see the issue so clearly – that Jesus is the only way to God – but it seems as though many of the people I talk to are in a fog and just can't see the truth. This is especially true of those who are involved in New Age thinking because religions blur into a sort of pluralistic oneness under the mantra of 'All is God, All is One and All ways lead to God.'

New Age

I was at a New Age Festival in London, called 'Mind, Body and Spirit'. The day had been busy and I was tired. Our Christian stall was like an island in a sea of occult confusion. For hours we had discussed spiritual things with Buddhists, spiritualists, witches and various seekers. Suddenly a couple stopped and looked very intently at our stall. I struck up a conversation with them. As the conversation developed I found that these people were extreme New Agers who seemed to have little grasp of reality. They just could not accept that anything was true or false, right or wrong. In desperation I asked them whether they thought that what Hitler had done to the Jews was right or wrong. With a sort of glazed expression one of them said, 'Everything is relative. It was all according to the spirit of the age.' With some patience I tried to use another example in order to build a foundation for a more meaningful dialogue. 'Is two plus two four?' I asked. 'It's all according to what you make it. You create your own reality,' came the reply. 'You mean that two plus two can be four, or seven or three thousand and six?' 'Yes, it is what you make it,' said the man. Exasperated I asked, 'Is the moon made of rock or blue cheese?' 'It's all according to what you think it is,' the woman answered. Looking at them in utter disbelief, I blurted out, 'But scientists came back with samples of moon-dust and moon-rock, not samples of cheese!' 'Ah,' exclaimed the man triumphantly, 'that's because the scientists were narrow-minded.'

Abdullah

I thank God that everyone I meet is not as confused and detached from reality. Abdullah came from a wealthy family in Somalia and was a devout Muslim. Being close to his grandfather who was a Sheik, he grew up with people travelling for many miles to come and visit this Islamic sage and teacher. It was in such an atmosphere of devotion to Islam that Abdullah became a very strong Muslim. He says, 'For me, Islam was the greatest and only religion and I was totally committed to my beliefs. I used to go to the mosque five times a day and by the age of fourteen I could recite the whole Quran from memory.'

In 1991, the civil war broke out in Somalia and Abdullah fled with his wife and children to refugee camps in Kenya. It was there that he came across aid workers who were Christians. The kindness shown by them, as well as by the Red Cross workers in Somalia, make him reconsider his distorted view of Christianity. He had been taught to regard Christianity as the religion of Satan, and yet 'Satan' was caring for his family whilst his rich Saudi Muslim brothers did nothing. As people were dying in the refugee camps Abdullah, wanting a better life for his family, managed to pay the cost of their flight to London. That was where we met.

When we discovered that they had virtually nothing, we managed to supply the family's needs in practical ways. Abdullah was constantly amazed that the 'Great Satan' could do such things. A wonderful friendship developed and he was very curious about the Bible and the Christian faith. We would often sit at the table for up to three hours studying the Scriptures. Even when he was a Muslim he knew more about the Bible than many Christians. My friend came regularly with his family to the Centre and watched as several 'big, bad men', as he called them, became Christians and were changed. Answers to prayer, and the fact that we could talk directly to God in an intimate way, astounded him. During his time in our district, he had several dreams with biblical meanings. Once he saw himself outside our house, with his nose pressed against the window, peering at the wonderful meal the Christians inside were enjoying. He knew that he had only to ask Christ to take away his sins and become his Lord and Saviour, and then he too, could join us in God's blessings.

After about a year, the family moved to another part of London, where I put them in touch with a good church. There the Christians put into practice the command to love their neighbours, helping the family in many practical ways. Again Abdullah saw miracles in answer to the prayers of God's people. Finally, melted by God's love and astounded at God's miraculous power, my friend became a Christian and today he is a great blessing in his church. He says, 'If Muhammad had no certainty of a place in heaven, what hope is there for any Muslim? But with Jesus there is the certainty of eternal life.'

Julian and Alison

Sometimes in my work, for God's own reasons, unusual things happen. I was visiting homes door to door in Enfield and speaking about my faith to others as I went. All of a sudden I had a strong vision of a particular flat in another street. Sensing that this was from God, I skipped several streets and went to the flat. When I rang the bell a young man with his arm in plaster came to the door. I told him I was from the local Christian Centre. He looked me up and down and asked, 'Are you a Jehovah's

Witness?' 'No,' I replied. 'Are you a Mormon, then?' 'No,' came my answer. 'Are you one of those 'born again' Christians?' 'I am a Christian who believes that you must be born again to know God,' I said. 'Oh, that's all right,' smiled the man. 'Come in!'

Julian, I discovered, had been involved in an accident whilst playing football, which explained why he had his arm in plaster. He had plenty of time to discuss spiritual things and he was like a sponge soaking up truth. Every week I met with him to discuss the Bible and eventually he prayed, turned from his self-reliance to earn his ticket to heaven and accepted Jesus as his own Saviour and Lord. His wife Alison did not take kindly to the nuisance of a 'religious nut' intruding into her nest and trying to 'brainwash' her husband. Week by week Julian and I sat at the table discussing the Bible while she glared at us with dark eyes in between watching television programmes with their children.

As the weeks passed I noticed that the glares softened and I often caught Alison listening intently to our conversations. When she saw me looking, she would bury herself in the television set again, only to re-emerge with hope in her eyes. There came a time when she joined Julian and me at the table and she too received the Saviour. God restored their marriage and he has since worked through them in a wonderful way, using them to bring others to Christ. They are now part of a church and a great benefit to it as they reach out to others and help many people.

While missionaries will spend many hours with those who want their company, they will not pursue those who make it clear they want to be left alone, though they will pray for them.

Lorna

When Lorna ran away to London she was sixteen years old and pregnant. Scared to tell her parents what had happened, she took what she thought was the easy option and left her home in the central belt of Scotland by the overnight bus to London. On arriving in the capital she saw an advertisement for a pregnancy centre in the ladies' toilet in the bus station and found her way there. An abortion was arranged and carried out, and when Lorna left the clinic she joined London's young homeless people. She made friends with two other girls and while they didn't spend their days together they looked out for each other at night. Lorna despised the beggars she saw on the streets and was determined to find a job and get out of the mess she was in. But that was easier said than done. Most people didn't want to employ someone with no fixed address, and those who did were offering jobs that Lorna wasn't prepared to consider. She was vulnerable, especially as she was traumatized after the abortion and had developed a real fear of men. Before she realized what was happening she slipped into a lesbian relationship with one of her two friends. There was a furious row over that and the third girl left. Lorna and Phoebe were penniless and homeless, but at least they were together.

It was when she was sheltering from pouring rain that Lorna first met a London City Missionary who had to pass her to get into a block of flats. The missionary made a friendly comment about the weather and went inside. When she discovered the girl still in the doorway as she left, the missionary stopped to talk. The floodgates opened and the young Scot poured out her story. Despite her relationship with Phoebe she was deeply lonely. Realizing this, the missionary invited her back to the Christian Centre to dry out her clothes and have a cup of tea. That was the first of many visits. To start with Lorna steered clear of any mention of the Christian faith. She had been brought up in a churchgoing home and had attended Youth Fellowship right up until she left home. Any talk of Christianity seemed painful for her and the missionary wondered if the subject made her homesick.

Heartbroken

For some months that situation continued, but one day, after an unusually long absence, Lorna arrived at the Christian Centre in a very distressed state. Phoebe had moved on. Despite protestations of undying love just a short time before, Phoebe had found a new partner and dropped her friend like a hot potato. Lorna was devastated. The girl needed to be needed, and without someone close who needed her she was totally lost. In her distress she got drunk, something she had never done before, and she despised herself for it. She was also taken up with morbid thoughts about her abortion and about the baby who might have been. In her loneliness it seemed to her that the baby would have been the one person who would have really needed her and who would never have left her. She felt so guilty that her mental state became a concern to the missionary. Suggestions of seeking medical help did not go down well, and the missionary gave what support she could as a friend. Gradually the dark cloud that enveloped Lorna began to lift and one day the girl asked about the Sunday service in the Christian Centre. Much to the missionary's delight the girl turned up there the following Sunday.

Things seemed to get better from then on. Lorna was at the service most Sundays and she opened up in a way she had never done before, even asking questions about the Christian faith, especially about God's offer to remove the guilt of those who trusted in him. She recognized that her guilt was dragging her down and that she needed to be rid of it. The missionary spent many hours with Lorna and had real hopes that she would become a Christian. She was so different; she stood taller and was more relaxed and assured and even talked about getting in touch with her parents to let them know that she was fine.

On the last occasion Lorna was at the service there was no indication that anything was wrong. Consequently, when she didn't turn up for two or three weeks, the missionary didn't feel unduly concerned, thinking that she might even have gone north to see her parents. But one day, when she was out visiting, the missionary saw Lorna. Their eyes met, and the young Scot turned and walked away with her companion, whom the missionary recognized as Phoebe. The missionary has seen Lorna many times since then but their eyes have never met. She still prays for her.

My earliest memories are of my childhood home in Ghana where I lived with my parents, brothers and sisters. There were seven of us in our family. Although my family went to church we were really from an animist background. My father's youngest sister was married to a palmist, and when we were born she was called to read our palms. Despite being nominally Christian my parents still bowed before their African gods, asking them to do things for them that the Lord didn't seem to be doing. In a dark room in our family house there was a little stool on which a god was supposed to sit, though there was nothing to be seen.

I was a twin, but my twin brother died. In my tribe, if you lost a twin brother or sister, a wooden image (a carved doll) was sculpted to represent the dead twin and the surviving twin carried it around everywhere with him. If a family lost both twins then two images were made. As a small boy I could not go anywhere without the image of my brother. When I ate, I sat it in front of me and put a few grains of rice or whatever food I was having beside it before I took my own. The image was such a part of me that if it was damaged I felt that hurt in my own body; if an arm was broken I felt pain at the very point of breakage.

Spiritual things were all around me in my childhood. There were sorcerers and magicians in our village who 'channelled the spirits', read tarot cards and carried out other occult practices. Voodoo was part of our village life. In fact, it is believed that it originated in my tribe. Voodoo did not do much good to people; rather its gods exacted judgement. For example, if a man who had money stolen thought he knew who had taken it, he would go to the fetish place where the fetish priest would give him the sum of money that had been stolen. Then the priest would go to the person who was thought to have stolen it asking for the money and for animal sacrifices to be made. If he did not, or could not, refund the money and provide the sacrifices, members of his family would be afflicted by sickness, even death.

Who am I?

Ancestral worship was also practised. When a baby was born, people believed that an ancestor had returned to earth through the baby and tried to find out which ancestor it was. I asked my mother who had come back in me, but she was not inclined to tell me. When someone died people made great efforts to establish the cause of death in order to know whether the dead person had gone to peace or torment. I remember after a funeral a man went into a trance and spoke. It was thought that the person we had buried was speaking through him. The voice was just like the dead person's voice; I knew it and recognized it. It didn't surprise us that a dead person spoke as many villagers talked to the dead.

Ancestors played a big part in our lives because we believed that they watched over us. When I was growing up, if anyone was taking a journey, he put on special clothes then gathered a gourd of water, a gourd of maize meal mixed with water, and a glass of the local strong palm spirit for a pot libation. Standing in front of his house he poured the maize meal in three directions on the ground, then did the same with the water and the spirit, so offering food and drink to his ancestors whom, he believed, would therefore guide him on his journey, help him to do his business, then bring him safely home. If a person's home was broken into when he was away, he called upon his ancestors, complaining to them that his goods had been stolen, and prayed that they would exact punishment on the thieves.

Pick and mix religions

Although my family went to church we were also involved in the spirit world. We lived in a mix of thinking. The perception was that the church preached the white man's god and the rest we inherited from our ancestors. Christianity and spiritism were held together by many people. The local brand of Catholicism didn't help matters; even the priests practised pot libations. People believed that spirits would do for us what God did not. For example, if someone became ill and prayed for healing but did not get better, he went to a witchdoctor or fetish priest who told him the cause of his illness, gave him herbs to take and rituals to perform. If the person recovered, people believed that these things had worked. It seemed to us that God was not in a rush to do things, and if we wanted a quick answer or a speedy recovery we should go to the witchdoctor or fetish priest, as we thought that the gods worked through them. Those of us who thought we were Christians believed the Lord worked through sorcerers too. As a result it was no big deal for so-called Christians to dabble in the spirit world.

As teenagers we were very interested in spiritual things and explored all sorts of occult practices. Being aware of the darkness that surrounds some kinds of black magic, we wanted an enlightened form of the occult, searching for information on such things as the lost books of the Bible and certain books of the Apocrypha. We also tried to invoke not only ancestors but also saints like St Anthony of Padua. There were rituals attached to him and to other saints and we went through them all carefully, longing to touch the supernatural, thinking that would make us powerful and give us a great deal of money. But nothing ever really happened. Looking back I can see that it was the Lord who saved me from becoming more deeply involved in these things.

The appeal of secrecy

In 1980, my older brother went to England

to do a marine engineer's course. When he came back to visit us in Ghana he and I used to sit for hours talking and reading about spiritual things, especially New Age thinking and Freemasonry. A picture that I saw in a newspaper of Isaac Newton who discovered the law of gravity when he saw an apple falling fascinated me. The article described him as one who had touched the supernatural, a man so open to the things of the spirit that the law of gravity was revealed to him. The article said that he was a Rosicrucian (the word means the rose cross), a member of an ancient order of Freemasonry. The secrecy around Freemasonry really appealed to us, but God kept us from becoming more deeply involved because we were not of a high enough class to be welcomed in. Our search continued elsewhere, even reaching the stage of sacrificing chickens to the spirits, though we were so poor that we had to stop. My brother ordered a book from India about magical eastern powers from ancient times in which there was a section on precious stones and the energy and power that was meant to flow from them; it fascinated us. We just got deeper and deeper into anything connected with the supernatural but, though things excited us at the time, nothing satisfied us for more than a short while.

Good news at last

When my brother next returned from England he told me that he had found what we were looking for. This was his story. He was on a boat that was visited by the pastor of a church near Bristol who told my brother about the Lord Jesus Christ in a way that was quite different from anything he had heard before. When I heard his testimony the reality of the Lord came to me for the first time. The light had never shone before. Because he was just a young Christian he felt he could not lead me to the Lord. Instead, he directed me to a Baptist Church and I went there the following Sunday.

I will never forget that service as the pastor spoke right into my mind and heart, almost as though my brother had gone to see him and told him all that we had talked about and all that I'd been thinking. At the end of the service, the pastor asked anyone who wanted to receive forgiveness and accept Jesus Christ as Lord and Saviour to come to the front of the church. I stood up, walked forward and knelt down and prayed. Realizing I needed to be forgiven, I knew in my heart that was not possible apart from the Lord Jesus Christ and that without him my life would be meaningless. I had looked for meaning for so long and suddenly I was certain about where it could be found. From then on I was different, God changed me and is still changing me today. When I became a Christian I sensed that the Holy Spirit was showing me that carrying the image of my dead twin brother was idolatry. Having dug a hole and buried the wooden thing, I felt freer than I'd ever felt before. Dad thought it was just a phase I was going through, but I'm glad to say that it was not.

I started getting up in the dark at 4 a.m. to pray. Dad was always up early because he ran a bakery. Mum, who knew I was praying in the mornings, joined me some months later and I had the pleasure of leading her to the Lord. After another eight months, at a time when things were not going well in the bakery because there was a shortage of flour, Dad also joined us and we prayed together. Soon afterwards we had the blessed privilege of leading Dad to Christ. Before they were converted Dad and Mum thought it was alright to go to sorcerers and diviners to have the future read, seeing such practices as part of the old religions. When they became Christians they realized that the only way to God is through Jesus Christ and that the Bible is against people contacting spirits. I am so thankful that God opened our eyes to know that spiritism is from the devil and delivered us from it.

My brother, who had gone back to the UK, sent us books explaining the error of our ways and showing us that these things were contrary to God's ways. Also we attended a church where the pastor preached against Satanism and encouraged us to read the Bible where it makes it quite clear that Satanism is wrong. We discovered that much of our thinking had been wrong. For example, we had believed in reincarnation, whereas the Bible teaches that we are created individually. Coming from a spiritist background meant that I carried a load of baggage into my new Christian life, but the Lord took that burden from me.

What next?
In the time that followed, having prayed fervently to the Lord asking him to open the door for me to study, an opportunity arose to take a course in England. I grasped

the opportunity and came to the UK, where for two years I attended Hampstead Bible College. As I felt that the Lord wanted me to be involved in looking after people I prayed that he would show me his will. What kept coming into my mind was the fact that French-speaking countries surround Ghana while Ewe, my tribal language, is only spoken in parts of four of them. I thought that the Lord might want me to study French in order that I could help spread the gospel in these countries. All my mind and heart was for foreign mission. For two years I studied French in England with a view to going back home. During that time I read that the population of the world was 5.2 billion people. My heart was burdened for them and I prayed that God would involve me in the salvation of souls. Perhaps that was a naive prayer.

Ama

When I was studying at Bible college, I went to a south London church one Sunday. There was a young Ghanaian woman there. 'I can't quite place you,' I told her, 'but I'm sure we've met before.' 'Which church do you go to in Accra?' she asked. I told her. 'Do you know Cecelia?' asked the young woman. 'She went to that church and her name is the same as yours.' I told her that Cecelia was my older sister! Then I remembered how we met. Three years previously, my older sister sang in a church choir that was asked to be the host choir for a week at a conference in Accra, the capital of Ghana. After one of the sessions I went to find my sister to let her know that I had appreciated her singing. I wanted to hug her and tell her that the singing had been very good. When I found her, she was with a young lady. My sister introduced us; her name was Ama. And now Ama and I had met again. We were married in 1995.

One day, in a Christian bookshop in Oxford Street, London, I was glancing at magazines and came across an advertisement saying that London City Mission was looking for evangelists and missionaries. I felt I just had to answer the advertisement. As I went through the selection process I had my own plans and understanding of what I wanted to do. But God led me in his way, not mine, and I found that even my naive prayer had been answered. Having prayed that the Lord would involve me in the work of salvation of the 5.2 billion people in the world, he took me to London where all the world can be found. Instead of travelling around the globe, I didn't have to move from London. My first assignment was at Brixton and as I visited round the doors there I met people from many countries, even some who spoke French. It was fun to try my French with them and to get it together again. From Brixton we moved to Lewisham where I found no French people at all. Lewisham was an interesting place for me because I met many Asian people and they helped to inform me about their culture and religious beliefs.

Under fire

Ama and I have two little boys, Edem and Delanyo. Edem means, 'God has delivered me', and Delanyo means, 'God is good'. We now live in Tottenham and are familiar with the problems the local people face from day to day. It is an inner city area and all the inner city problems are there: drug and alcohol addiction, unemployment and prostitution. Some people in the area have a problem with racism, but it has never really been an issue with me. From time to time when I'm doing door-to-door visitation things are said that could be hurtful.

Occasionally I've been told to go back to the jungle I came from. My response is that it is God who made me and who brought me here; he gave me this work to do and if anyone has a problem with that they should speak to him about it rather than to me. I'm only doing what he tells me. Knowing that my identity is from God takes the strain out of situations like that. If I regarded myself as someone special then when insulted, I'd feel bad about it. But that's not how it is. These attacks are not against me but against God who made me who I am, made me look as I do, and gave me this work to do for him. Only the Lord is important when I knock on someone's door; I am not. Sometimes I wonder what I would be doing if the Lord had not saved me – I might have been in prison by now. I remember that when I'm speaking to people, especially any who are unpleasant to me.

Door-to-door visitation is a wonderful privilege. I met a young man on the doors and we got talking. Having shared my testimony with him, telling him how I became a Christian, I told him about the Lord and what he meant to me. The young man said that he'd never heard it like that before and he too became a believer. He has been coming to our services for about two years now, never missing one. Being a missionary is hard work, but when people are converted it seems so worthwhile.

As well as door-to-door visitation we have a full programme of events at the Siddons Christian Centre in Tottenham. We run a food bank, collecting food and helping support people with it, because although some of the area look fairly upmarket, it is really quite a poor part of London. Saving money on food allows people to repay some of their debts. Nearly everyone in the area is in debt; that's a really big problem. We also run a club for senior citizens at which our oldest member is ninety-one. There we play games and generally enjoy ourselves, then read the Bible and I share God's Word. The Centre also takes the opportunity to reach out to teenagers though a club each Monday where we play games and have a time of sharing about the Lord. The teenagers come with many questions which we try to answer. Children are not left out either because we run a club for them, right down to five-year-olds. I love to see their faces when we are talking about Jesus. Ama is also involved with the work of the Mission, teaching in

Sunday School and helping with teas for our meetings. Sometimes she also helps with the clubs. On Sundays we have a service at the Centre and the people who come really seem to enjoy it. I do too as it allows me to talk to them about the Lord. Jesus Christ has done so much for me, bringing me out of all the sinfulness of my heart and leading me into the truth that is only to be found in him, that I just love telling others about him.

I just love them!

Many people seem to appreciate the work the Mission does even if they don't agree with it, but some don't and we have had one or two difficult times. When I was a new missionary we met with some unpleasantness that was like a baptism to show me exactly what I should expect. It discouraged me for a short time before I remembered that the Bible is full of people who were persecuted for their faith. What happened to us was not persecution, but it made me feel under fire. For example, we have had several attempted break-ins. Once when my wife was in the kitchen someone tried to open the skylight and get in. I was away with the car and that made the place look empty. There are regular break-ins in the area and what happened to us helps us to better understand what other people are going through. I just love the people and my heart goes out to them. So many of those we meet live in a torn world, waking up each morning with no structure to the new day because they are out of work. I thank God each morning for putting us where we are, for allowing us the opportunity of befriending the people round about us, and for opening doors to tell them about our Saviour. It's a great privilege to hold out hope to people who feel hopeless.

God has done a wonderful thing through the work of the Mission in Tottenham, bringing some people into new life in him. An 88-year-old man, whose wife came to the Centre, never came with her. It was only when she died that we discovered that he didn't even know she attended! When she did pass away I went to be with him and their children for the funeral. Afterwards I asked him if he would like to come along and be part of our Tuesday programme where he would meet a dozen or so people about his own age. The first time he came he was a little unsure, but the following week he asked if I could give him a lift to the Sunday service. After coming to the service for two months he asked the lady who was working with me at the Centre to share the gospel of the Lord Jesus Christ with him. My colleague visited twice a week after that and I visited weekly. The Lord gave her opportunities to talk to him about Jesus and one day our elderly friend surrendered his life to the Saviour. That was on a Wednesday; the following Sunday he stood up at the service and testified to the saving grace of Jesus.

When I think back over my life I know how much I have to thank God for. I was absolutely lost in the occult and so-called New Age practices, finding no hope in any of them. The interesting thing about New Age thinking is that it's not new at all. Much of it is based on traditional religions from Africa and the East. I know from my own experience what they involve and that there is absolutely no good news in them. The only good news is Jesus. He has saved my soul and I'll serve him with all my heart until the day I die and go home to him in heaven.

Every few months I visited Ada Lee, but had never met her son Stan, whom I knew to be a drug addict. Her parting shot was always, 'You've got a meeting for women down at the Centre?' 'Yes, we have,' I assured her. 'It's on Thursdays and you're very welcome to come.' 'I'll be there,' she would say. 'I'll see you there.' It took her ages to appear at the meeting, but the Thursday came when she did. Then she started coming on Sundays too. One Sunday her son Stan arrived at his mother's flat and found the door locked. It was a cold night and, rather than hang about and get chilled, he came into the service where he knew he would find her. Wearing a dirty red velvet jacket and with long greasy hair he ambled right to the front of the meeting and sat down. I knew who he was, guessed why he was there, and preached my heart out because I thought he might never hear about Jesus again.

Stan

Stan was one of my surprises because he did come back, and soon he came along to our Bible study meeting too. We often talked together, especially about a book on which he was very keen that suggested that Jesus was not God but an astronaut. One night Stan came to me in a serious mood. 'Have you got anything that will help me get into God?' he asked. I gave him a Bible Study course and through it he became a Christian. There was no drama in Stan's coming to the Lord, just a quiet birth into faith. At that time I was involved in hospital chaplaincy work and through it I got Stan a portering job.

After his conversion Stan came off drugs. Although that was hard for him, it wasn't as hard as it is for some people because he had a phobia of needles and would only take what he could smoke or pop. He wasn't into injecting at all and that kept him off heroin or crack. It was a joy watching Stan growing in the Lord over the years that followed. His whole lifestyle changed; he looked different too. Some time after his conversion he came to me. 'I want to get married,' he told me. I assured him that I'd pray that God would send Miss Right. He did. Stan and Miss Lesley Wright met and were married! Stan's mother has since died and gone to be with the Lord.

But life was not always a bundle of joys for Stan, even after he was converted and free of drugs. At one time he was plagued with fears, probably to the point of paranoia. After a particularly bad episode, he told me what had happened. 'I was frightened, like really frightened, and I prayed. And suddenly it was as if God was just hugging me and my fear went away.'

A way with words
There is real depth in Stan, and sometimes he expresses it best in poetry. Many times he has arrived at our home and either Anne or I have typed his poems for him. They are both Christian and secular, and all of them are moving in their own way. Stan is different; he's not just your average guy. Seeing him converted and growing more like Jesus has been a great thrill to both Anne and me over the years we have known him. Occasionally he has even helped us in our work, doing door-to-door visiting with us. That was great, for he knew the people in the area and, despite a fair degree of deafness, he was able to talk to them about

the Lord who had saved him from his sin and addiction and who would love him to the end.

Harry

Door-to-door visiting didn't always have as happy an ending. In the early years of my work as a missionary Anne and I used to go round the doors together; that was before our children were born. A young woman welcomed us into her flat one day, though it turned out afterwards that it was my Yorkshire accent that attracted her, not anything we said about the Lord. When we entered we found several people there, all as laid back as you like. Shortly after we arrived another guy, Harry, came in. But as soon as he saw us he made a bolt for the door. His sister laughed and yelled after him, 'It's OK. It's not the Old Bill.' I suppose my height, my black leather jacket and my wife next to me, made us look like plain-clothes detectives! Harry came back, grinning. The atmosphere was so relaxed that we were able to talk to the people there about the Lord. We gave them gospels before leaving, never realising that the laid back little group we had left were drugged up to the eyeballs.

Breaking bail

One day Harry's wife banged on our door. 'I can't handle this any more,' she wailed, when we took her in. 'Men have been to the door and held a gun at Harry's head.' That kind of thing wasn't all that unusual when drugs were involved. Their situation was dire, and Harry was no stranger to the courts. When on bail, in the early days we knew him, he persuaded a friend who was as hard up as he was to stand bail for him; then Harry broke his bail conditions, heading out of the country with his wife and children. He didn't like where they went and, leaving the family there, he headed back to England, only to miss the train to London. Anyone else on bail would have kept their head down, but Harry created a scene and the police were called. It didn't take long for them to recognize who he was and arrest him, thankfully before the court had called on his friend to pay up. That was a real answer to prayer because his friend was also a good friend of ours!

Things looked better for Harry for a short time when he went into a drug rehabilitation centre. While he was there and free of drugs he made a commitment to the Lord. Unfortunately it was a smoke-free establishment and, when they discovered that he was still on the weed, he was kicked out. Then life took a turn for the worse. Harry was involved in a drug deal that went wrong and ended up being charged with attempted murder. Despite the victim saying Harry wasn't guilty, he was imprisoned, but not for long. The judge had misdirected the jury and he was released on that technicality.

In my efforts to befriend and help Harry I got into some serious scrapes, so much so that I had to take legal advice. One day, when he was on the run, I had him in the car. We'd met at his sister's flat and he'd asked to come to a Bible study with me. On our way to the meeting we came across an accident. A girl had been knocked down on a crossing. As nobody was with her, I got out of the car to see if I could help until the police arrived. By then my car was blocking the movement of traffic. Police or no police, and despite being banned from driving, Harry moved the car then came and stood beside me. A crowd began to gather and the constable moved the people back, leaving me still cradling the girl. 'What are you doing?' he asked Harry. 'I'm with the vicar,' Harry told him, not moving away even though he was on the run. After the incident was cleared, he and I headed for the Bible study meeting. 'Has anyone anything they want to share with the others?' the leader asked, in the course of the evening. Harry spoke out. 'You know,' he said, 'I try to serve God but I find it almost impossible to do. Please pray for me.' He was weeping.

Opposite extremes

That wasn't the only time we prayed for Harry, far from it. He was tested in prison, found to be HIV positive, and spent some time in hospital really quite ill. The people at the Christian Centre prayed fervently that the Lord would heal him. Weeks later I went to see him and found him in a furious mood. 'You'll never guess what's happened!' he spat out. 'I've been back to the hospital and I'm clear of HIV. The first test wasn't right and I've been living in fear all these months. I'm going to take the lot of them to court and sue them for all I can get!' There was no thankfulness and no thought that God might have healed him.

Harry's reaction could not have been more different from Frank's. He was a prisoner in Belmarsh who asked to see me. 'I'm HIV positive,' he told me, 'and I'm going to have to tell my girlfriend.' I prayed for him there and then and kept on praying on his behalf, asking the Lord to heal and bless him and his girlfriend. Later Frank had another test and was found to be clear. He wasn't angry because he saw it as answered prayer. Our phone rang one day some time afterwards. 'I thought you'd like to know,' Frank's voice said, 'I've met a nice girl. We're married and we're going to church. I'm phoning to tell you that I've just been baptized.'

Trevor

Drug addiction doesn't only affect addicts; it impacts their families too. We had a lot of contact with a couple that clocked up enormous drug bills. Even when the husband was in prison he would get supplies through a dealer, which meant on release he was up to the eyes in debt. They were so broke that they gave Trevor, their two-year-old son, to his Aunt Jean and Uncle Robert who were also addicts. The boy lived with them until he was teenager. Sadly, he was involved in a life of crime before he knew what the word crime meant.

When Trevor was just a little boy of about eight, he was trained to take a cup in his

hand and knock the doors around his home.
If a door was answered he said that his aunt
had sent him to borrow a cup of sugar. If
there was no reply he went home, told his
uncle, and the place was broken into and
burgled. Another of his jobs was emptying
the ashtrays if someone came to the door.
That might seem harmless enough, but it
was not. The visitor might be the police and
the ashtrays would certainly be filled with
doped fag ends. I was so worried about the
boy that I spoke to the NSPCC and social
services, but he was left in that environment.
Around the same time someone reported
to the RSPCA how Trevor's aunt and uncle
treated their dog, and the dog was removed.
Trevor has grown up now, and he's in and
out of prison, following in the family
tradition.

Having been farmed out by his parents
as a two-year-old, Trevor is now without his
uncle and aunt too. I visited them over the
years, and Robert never spoke, leaving that
to Jean. But when he was in prison he asked
to see me. 'I've been converted,' Robert
told me happily, 'and I want Jean to become
a Christian.' I took her to an evangelistic
campaign and she made a commitment to
the Lord. Sadly, when Robert was released,

it all went pear-shaped in ways too complex to describe. They both went back on drugs and Robert was imprisoned, yet again. One day he was found hanging in his cell. Despite that terrible end to his life, I'm sure Robert was a Christian and that I'll meet him one day in heaven. Jean, poor Jean, is also dead. She got into a drunken stupor, inhaled her own vomit and died.

Over my years as a missionary I have had real encouragements. Stan was one of them, Frank another. I've been given some hope that others were converted, even though things might seem different to those who don't know the full details of their situation. That's why I hope to see Robert in heaven, and maybe Jean, and maybe Harry. But there have been many Trevors. I've told each one of them the good news that there is life in Jesus Christ and forgiveness of sins, all their sins, but I can't take the step of acceptance for them. I've got to leave that up to them. But I keep on praying.

Janet George

When my brother and I were children, my parents sent us to Sunday School and as we grew older we went to church. My brother became a Christian, but I just liked the emotional side of going to church rather than taking it seriously and making any kind of commitment to God. Sadly, when he was converted, my parents became quite anti-religion though they didn't give me a hard time for attending church. They probably knew I wasn't as committed as my brother. I was going though the teenage stage when he left home and I went off the rails a bit. At least, that's what my parents thought. They didn't like me going to parties and coming home late. I didn't smoke or take drugs; I just went out and enjoyed myself. Until I was twenty-three I continued to live at home, but by then I felt I wanted to be more independent. Also my parents didn't like the West Indian boy I was going out with at the time. That relationship caused a lot of problems. I left home, shared various bed-sits and houses with friends, and continued to enjoy my partying. In between times I went back to stay with my parents.

Eventually the council offered me a bed-sit in Hackney in Hoxton. My parents seemed quite happy about that and Dad helped to decorate the place. I liked living there, enjoying my independence and not having to answer to anyone if I came in late or had too much to drink. But I began to feel that God was speaking to me about the way I was living. Sometimes I woke up during the night feeling really frightened, convinced that I was going to hell if I went on the way I was going. From the teaching I'd had at Sunday School and church I knew I wasn't living the right way. Occasionally I had terrible nightmares all about hell but I tried to ignore them and get on with my life. There was nobody I could talk to about my fear of hell, and it was always there at the back of my mind. Although I knew I should do something about it, I kept putting it off.

Facing facts
About 1978 things came to a head and I could not avoid the issue any longer. At the time I was going out with a married man and it wasn't a good relationship at all. I tried to finish with him but he wouldn't give up. Some nights he banged on my door and called through my letterbox which, because I was on my own, could be very frightening. For months he kept ringing me. That was a difficult time because I knew that if I didn't break off the relationship I wouldn't be able to get right with God. I continued resisting him, and in the end he left my life.

Eventually one evening I went along to the Mission in Hoxton. It was just up the road from where I lived. I didn't know which door to go to and I chose the wrong one. I knocked but there was no answer. But as I was determined to get in I went down to the basement and tried the door there, but it was closed. While I was wondering what to do next the missionary, David Linley, came round the corner. He was very friendly and he took me into the Centre and down to a room where a small group of people had met for the evening service. I think I made a commitment to God after I went home that night. And I had also made a commitment to change. The next morning was amazing. I had a wonderful joy. I felt happier than I'd ever felt before. It was as though a great burden had been lifted from me. And the cloud that had hung over me for years had gone. I'll never forget that day.

After that I went to the evening service every Sunday and my life did change. Before I became a Christian, I sometimes read my Bible and tried to pray, but the Bible made no sense and I didn't think anyone was listening to my prayers. Suddenly the Bible became real. I bought daily reading

notes to help me understand it better.
Scripture really is God's Word and he speaks
through it. The sermons were simple and
not full of jargon. David Linley and his wife
Anne took me under their wing and were
very kind to me. The other people at the
Mission were friendly too and I felt at home
with them. Some time later, I got to know
Colin. He had been going to the Mission
for years. He was one of those who stood at
the door before the service to welcome
people in. We got chatting and, because
there was only an evening service at the
Mission, he asked if I would like to go with
him to the morning service at the East
London Tabernacle at Mile End. Colin
started taking me over there and I found
the services helpful. Although we went to
East London Tabernacle, we were still
involved in the work of the Mission.
Because I remembered things I'd learned
when I was young, I was keen to help in
Sunday School. It was a privilege to teach
six little three- to five-year-olds about my
Saviour and I hoped and prayed that they
would come to him too. I believe that God
led me into this work after I read in the Bible
that he gives us gifts and we should use
them. That's what I felt I was doing in

Sunday School. I also went to the Young People's Club.

Colin and I had a platonic relationship then but eventually we started going out together. For the next four years we got to know each other as we worked together and worshipped together at the Mission and the Tabernacle. Eventually I moved to the Tabernacle and became a member there. Colin had a difficult time then because his father was dying of cancer. But in 1982 he proposed to me and we were married. That was a happy and sad occasion because Colin's dad died just three days before our wedding. Since then we've been members of the East London Tabernacle and very involved there. I've never once regretted becoming a Christian. Jesus is my best friend and the church is my family.

Not always easy
Some people think that Christians have easy lives. I know that's not true. We had hoped to have children but were not able to. That was difficult at first and I questioned God though I don't think I was angry with him, just sad and disappointed. There was a lot going on in our lives at that time because when we were having infertility

investigations my dad became very ill. The stress was all too much for me and I had a breakdown. In a strange way that was the time in my life when God seemed closest to me. I was in hospital for three weeks and Jesus kept me company. That was a bad patch but it was also very special because I was so aware of God's presence.

When Colin was in his late forties he had a triple bypass, but the operation wasn't a complete success though he does manage to work. And two years ago I had cancer. Although it was a terrible shock God was really with us through that time and our friends at church prayed for us and supported us. So it is not our experience that Christians have an easy life. We have the same trials and tribulations as everyone else. What is different is that God is with us whatever happens. I don't know how people cope with life's problems and worries if they don't believe in God. Colin and I know that whether we live or die we belong to Jesus and he will care for us.

Seven >> Ashley Trask

I was born in Sialkot, in Pakistan, but came to England in the early sixties when I was four or five years old. My parents thought Dad would be able to get a job here and that their children would have a better education than at home. I remember very little about Pakistan apart from driving for a long time through the mountains to catch the plane for London. We lived in the London Borough of Islington and I had all my schooling there. That could have been a difficult time for me as it was the skinhead era and Paki-bashing was a popular sport, but I didn't have much racism against me, probably because I didn't stand out. I wore the same clothes as everyone else and hung out with the right people. Even as a boy I was quite good at working out who the right people were. Also I didn't distance myself from other boys because I recognized that made me a sitting target. It wasn't deliberate, but I also began to talk cockney. I still do.

Ours was a Muslim family and I did just what Dad and Mum told me to do. That was what was expected of me. Although my parents told me about Allah and read the Quran to me, I just couldn't get a hold of what they were teaching me; I don't think I ever really knew their god at all. I suppose I was a nominal Muslim, but the religion meant nothing to me. Because Dad was very strict I wasn't allowed out much, and when I was allowed out I made sure he didn't hear what I got up to with my friends. If he had known some of our mischief I'd have suffered for it. My father used to take me to the mosque now and again, but it never meant anything to me. I took my shoes off like everyone else and I listened to what was going on, but it just didn't reach me. While I knew people were praying, I couldn't see who they were praying to. Who was listening? I said prayer words to someone Dad called Allah but I just couldn't get a grip of the thing. Allah wasn't there, wasn't tangible. Although I was in the mosque with the rest of them I felt very distant from everyone else and from what was going on around me. I don't remember much about it except that the mosque was very beautiful and that when you entered the prayer room you had to take off your shoes. The people there were very friendly and warm.

Missing out

Most days I went straight home from school because I had to help Dad in his second hand furniture shop. I did have some evenings off because I had a private teacher to help me with maths. As a family we did not celebrate birthdays or Christmas. Knowing that other kids did, I felt we were missing out on something special. I suppose we were really quite poor. Dad used to give me a good ticking off when I played football with the boys in primary school and got my shoes scuffed. At the time I thought he was just being heavy-handed, but I suppose it was because shoes cost money that he maybe didn't always have. Sometimes I envied my school friends and their designer clothes, record players and the like. I think Dad loved me though he never said so. He was very strict and would smack me hard when I was naughty. In a strange way I think that was how he showed his love: caring enough about me to punish me when I did something wrong.

A terrible time

In 1974, when I was fourteen, Dad developed lung cancer that spread to his liver. After a horrible illness he died at home. I have very vivid memories of his death. Mum was hysterical. I saw Dad's body lying on the bed. It was as though I was in the middle of a nightmare and couldn't wake up. I'd never really given much thought to death, and when Dad died I cried and cried inside myself. That was a terrible time. I still miss my dad. Mum was left with four children to bring up. I have three sisters, one older than me and two younger. When I was fifteen I left school to help Mum run the business. I was just a typical teenager from about the age of fourteen to eighteen, hanging around with my friends and going to pubs and parties. There is no law in Islam that says you can't go to parties, although some Muslims don't drink. But because I didn't believe in Allah I felt no need to keep the Muslim laws and started taking drink and drugs, enjoying that lifestyle a lot. My friends and I often went to the pictures and concerts, usually getting in without paying.

Most Saturdays they came to my house and we had a party. Mum hated it and was often mad with me. When she'd had enough of us she used to chase everyone out with a broom!

I suppose what made Mum mad was that she saw me getting deeper into that lifestyle and knew I'd get into real trouble eventually. I nearly did. One day when I was out with my friends, we smashed a car and pinched a load of golf balls and ice-skating stuff. Then we carried it all to my house and took the bricks out of our night store heater and hid what we'd stolen inside it. Next day the police came round, and that really got the wind up me. It turned out that they were investigating a murder and I fitted the description of the main suspect! When they discovered I had nothing to do with the murder they left me alone. That was a very distressing time for Mum and for me too. The friend I was with at the time of breaking into the car died some time ago. He was aged about 26. I often think of him and of how different our lives turned out.

A different journey

Because the area we lived in wasn't really a Muslim community there wasn't local pressure to conform to Islamic standards. Dad's death gave me freedom to go off on a different journey from his. I felt English and didn't get into Asian things at all. When I faced up to my background, which I tried to avoid doing, I actually hated myself for being an Asian, though I certainly didn't hate Asians, just me. I even supported England at cricket although my heart felt something for the Pakistan cricket team, especially if they were playing well!

A London City Missionary, whom we got to know because he visited a Greek family just along the road from us, came to our house sometimes. Mum didn't give me grief about his visits because she had other things on her mind. Those first years after Dad died must have been really hard for her but I didn't realize it at the time. The missionary left leaflets and invited us to go to the Christian Centre. Eventually I started going just to keep him happy and I read some of his leaflets too. They were quite interesting but I didn't read them with any real understanding. I liked the atmosphere at the Centre because the people were open and welcoming; that's why I kept going. I'd not experienced their kind of love and acceptance before, not even at the mosque.

I have to admit that the Christian Centre wasn't nearly as nice as the mosque.

We did a variety of different things at the Centre, but what I remember best was three films I saw there: *The Thief in the Night*, *The Cross and the Switchblade* and a Billy Graham film. Something in the films made me think, and what they made me think about was hell. The more I thought, the more scared I became. I definitely didn't want to go to hell. It was that fear that made me find out more about God and, when I was seventeen or eighteen, I became a Christian. The fear of hell went away then because I knew that Christians, when they died, went to heaven. One of the things I remember about that time is the joy there was in the Christian Centre when I was converted. People I thought were important took a real interest in me. That made me feel valued and did me good. At first much of the preaching didn't mean much but it grew on me.

Early struggles

For a couple of years after my conversion I had trouble with Mum. Although she was a nominal Muslim her religion meant enough to her that she was really upset I'd become a Christian. She even lost a number of friends over it. That bothered me, but it didn't make me want to give up my faith. After what seemed a long while my mother began to respect some of my Christian friends and when she was seriously ill she even let one of them pray for her. I'm afraid I wasn't a good example of a Christian because I tried to keep one foot in both worlds. For quite a long while I really struggled, moving from one job to another and not settling down to anything. Then, in 1985, I went to Capernwray Bible College for a year and became totally sold out for Jesus. I was so challenged by my time there that I wanted to serve God full-time from then on, though I didn't know how. At first that prospect really upset Mum but she came to accept it. My sisters were just relieved that I'd changed! The following year I worked with a church in Islington, then a friend selling packaging to the antique trade employed me. People asked me why I didn't consider working for London City Mission, but that didn't appeal to me even though it was through the Mission I'd been converted. I really wasn't sure what God wanted me to do.

Life as a London City Missionary
Eventually I did apply to LCM and was
accepted as a candidate. After my training
and probation I worked as an evangelist in
Limehouse, East London. I did door-to-
door visiting, helped in a drop-in centre,
organized a football club. I also visited pubs
to talk to people there, trained to be a lay
reader and married a curate! When I was
baptized I wanted to cut myself off from
my Islamic background and changed my
first name. Because of the racism in East
London, a few years after Marion and I
were married we took her name rather than
using mine. My work changed after four
years and I was appointed Borough Police
Chaplain working in South London. As
that's a pastoral job I spend much of my time
visiting police stations befriending staff and
officers and going out on shifts with boys
on the beat. More recently I've become a
special constable, which allows me to really
get alongside the officers and get to know
them as equals. Apart from it helping in
my work, being a special constable gives me
pleasure just for its own sake. I try to
socialize with the men too, going out for a
pizza or a curry and relaxing together. That
kind of contact makes it easier for people

to talk to me when they want to discuss problems or to talk about Christianity. The Lord has given me a real and deep desire to see the police officers coming to know him.

One day I was talking to a young officer in his mid-twenties; we were discussing fathers. I told him about my dad dying and how much I missed him. He shared his story. His father was violent towards him and he had never really experienced fatherly love. That young man's story gave me an opening to talk to him about God the Father and about the depth of his love for us. We were able to discuss personal Christianity, not just religious ideas. It's always a privilege to talk with others about the Lord and the healing he can bring about in our lives, not just healing of our human problems but healing of our sin-sick souls.

On fire for Jesus

Although I have cut my ties with Islam I have great respect for black and Asian people. They are a minority in the police force and sometimes they have a hard time, but I really like the contact I have with them. And black Christians are something else! I love their respect for the authority of God and his Word and their fervency for him is incredible. These folk are so totally out and out for Jesus and that's what I want to be. Their preaching is something else – it's on fire and it burns a way into my heart.

Tough times

People sometimes think that when you have a Christian home it is all 'Happy Families'. That's not been true for us, and I don't know anyone it is true for. Our two children, Christopher and Rebekah, are lovely, but our son has a health problem that controls much of what we can do as a family. We had a real struggle in lots of ways when we moved to work in Bermondsey, but God has even been able to use that. My job as a missionary is to try to share my faith and, if everything seemed all right with us, people might find us unapproachable. As it is, we have obvious problems and most people know that. In a strange way our circumstances allow folk to be real with us and us to be real with them. It seems implanted into some Christians that they have to be seen to be perfect; an attitude I believe does a lot of damage. I try not to pretend, even though that sometimes makes me feel a failure, but it does open the door for people to share their own troubles and burdens with me.

I suppose I have allowed myself to be vulnerable by sharing what my real feelings are, even when I'm angry, and any kind of injustice does make me angry. There have been times when God has seemed far away and I've shared that too. People then feel able to open up their own hearts. I have discovered that the more real I am with people, the more real they are with me. As I share deeply others do too. And it seems to be that I'm also now able to be more open with God. I try not to pretend with him. There is no point anyway as he knows exactly what's in my heart and in my mind. It is at times when I'm as honest as I can be with the Lord that he blesses me and I am most aware of his love and healing in my life.

Although I try not to pretend with other people, sadly sometimes I manage to fool myself. A few years ago, after preaching at church one Sunday, I phoned a friend and asked what he thought of the service. 'You were showing off,' he told me. 'You're looking for the praise and glory of men and you need to repent of that.' Another friend said the same. I was gutted. But after I'd thought about what they had said I knew it to be true. I told my minister that I didn't want to preach for a while. Maybe that seems a strange thing to print in a book, but it was an experience I'd not swap for anything. God reached out to me and showed me what I was becoming, a proud Christian, and a proud Christian sets himself up for a fall and is totally unworthy of being used in the Lord's service. That experience changed both me and my view of the work I do.

All part of life

Only once I've asked God why Christopher has all his health problems. Since then I think most of the time I've accepted that illness and other difficulties are all part of life and Christians live in the real world the same as everyone else. Marion and I cope differently. She is the thinker of the family, reacting with well thought-out answers. I just react with my feelings. We're a good combination. For both of us the bottom line is that God is good. We don't know why we have our problems but we're sure he has a reason for them and that the reason is good. In all our struggles God has been right there with us. We've learned important lessons through them, especially about forgiveness. And in the last few years we've begun to understand about the suffering and pain and the mixture of confusing emotions that come with them because we've met them ourselves. I believe God can heal our son, but I don't know if he will. And although I don't know what the future holds, I know God holds our future and I will trust him for that. Praise be to the God and Father of our Lord Jesus Christ!

Eight >> June Angelos

I was just three years old when my grandad died. Although far too young to understand what had happened, I remember the confusion and terrible upset I felt. Before he died I had spent a lot of time with my nan and grandad and everything seemed to go downhill when he wasn't any longer there. I'm told that I changed when he died, but his passing was probably not the only reason. Every childhood has its ups and downs, but my downs were perhaps deeper than many children go through. When the time came to go to secondary school I felt I'd reached the pits and I decided to block out all my misery by deliberately setting out to get drunk. I was eleven or twelve. And that same night I tried drugs for the first time. Anything that dulled my hurts and pains seemed worth any risk they brought with them.

The years that followed went from bad to worse, certainly as far as school was concerned. Drink and drugs were my ways of coping and when I was drunk or high it seemed like fun. Reality was different; I just grew more and more miserable. Although I was capable of doing well at school I didn't. When I was sixteen I left and went to college, but every new start I tried to make seemed blighted, and college was just more of the same. More unhappiness, more drink, more misery, more drugs. Eventually, feeling utterly broken, so much so that I didn't want to live, I took an overdose and hoped – really hoped - I would die. I collapsed in a field and had it not been for someone walking a dog, that might have been the end of me. Instead I found myself stuck for months in a psychiatric hospital, drugged up and despairing.

Developing a pattern

Even in hospital I was still a user, but when I moved into rehab that wasn't allowed. My life's pattern began to be established: in rehab I was free of drink and drugs, out I headed straight for the pub and the pusher. Because I was still under eighteen the first time I came out of rehab, I had the choice of going home or into the care system. I went home. At the time I was only aware of how awful life was for me; it was years later that I began to realize just what my condition did to the family. Much of the time I was suicidal and any thought of God enraged me. I read book after book disproving the existence of God, and I grew more and more anti God, anti religion, in fact anti anything that could begin to help me out of the mess I was in.

Somehow I managed to get one job after another over the next four years. Then a way out of the hole I was in seemed to present itself when a friend who was relocating to London asked me to move there with her. I was up and off. We found a flat and settled down to life in the capital. But, once again, it was just more of the same. I was still drinking, still using drugs, still looking for a way out. Several times I made attempts at suicide, sometimes more to try to escape than to die. But much of the time I didn't only want to die, I wanted never to have lived. Even as a child I remember feeling like that, wanting never to have been, never to have known hurt and pain and despair. I wanted my past unravelled and there to be nothing left of me when the last knot was undone, not even a memory of my having been. Phases passed, I took different drinks and experimented with different drugs, but the one thing that was constant, either at the back on my mind or as a consuming thought, was annihilation.

New flatmate

About two years after going to London we moved flats and needed another person to help pay the rent; and the girl who came to join us was a Christian. She moved in against the advice of the members of her church because our lifestyle was known in the area. However, this girl felt that if she did come God would use her to tell the rest of us about Jesus. In fact, she believed that somehow I would be saved. Each week the housegroup of which she was a member prayed for me. Her friends invited me to their homes for meals and talked to me despite what I was and all I did. Sometimes I really messed things us badly but they still treated me in the same kind way. Before then people had only wanted to know me when I was on a high but these girls accepted me however I was. When I first met them I thought they were off the wall! But their joy sometimes really got to me. Ours was a first floor flat, and I remember one night sitting in the lounge feeling utterly miserable. I'd been drinking and taking drugs and, because they operate on a law of diminishing returns, I didn't even get a high. My flatmate climbed the stair to the flat on her way home from a housegroup meeting, singing as she came in the door. Although I liked her I felt so, so angry that I could have picked her up and thrown her out the window. I'd spent good money on drink and drugs and was in despair, she'd spent nothing and was happy. How that enraged me!

Amazed!
When our flatmate decided to be baptized, she wanted us to go to the service. Eventually, and reluctantly, we agreed, thinking that we'd leave right after it and head for the pub. But when the night came, I became separated from the other two. They ended up safely in the gallery while I found myself sitting right at the front of the church. It was a very lively service, and I just sat there in total bewilderment at what was going on around me. My flatmates upstairs realized my discomfort and laughed at me. I don't remember a lot about the service, in

fact, there is a lot I don't remember from those days because I was so badly affected by my habit. What I do remember is that at the end of the service, when I got up to leave, people came to talk to me. I was amazed. That kind of thing just didn't happen to someone like me. The pastor, his wife and several others all talked to me, actually hung around specially to talk to me. One guy, he was covered in tattoos, told me his experience of being converted whilst in prison. He seemed to feel he had to keep talking to me, keep telling me about Jesus. As he talked, I suddenly found myself thinking that Jesus was real, and that either I believed in him right away or turned my back on any thought of him whatever. But I couldn't walk away. I just couldn't do it. There was so much I didn't understand, but that night I was sure of the reality of Jesus. That was over thirteen years ago.

Even as I was going back to the flat I found it hard to take in what had happened, whatever it was. The next day I tried to think it through. I'd done some awful things in the past; I knew that. And if God was real what had he made of my anti God thinking. Was this only an emotional high? Was I just having some kind of trip? For a week or two I thought it through from every different angle, doing mental somersaults and wondering if this part of the Bible or that part could be true. At the end of the struggle there was almost a sense in which I felt I didn't care. Things like that could be worked on and worked out in the future, I decided, it was enough for me to know that Jesus was real, really real and really powerful. I'd love to say that what followed was all peace and joy. But it wasn't. I started going to the housegroup meeting, then after some weeks I went to church. And I attended Alcoholics Anonymous and Narcotics Anonymous too. Their meetings really helped me as they kept me out of temptation, out of the pub. Because those who go know what others are going through, they really are supportive. Sadly, my best friend, who didn't like the changes in me and in my life, stopped having anything to do with me. That was hard.

Guilt

For two or three months of sheer desperate will power I fought to live what I thought was a Christian life. Though I still smoked cigarettes I took no drink or drugs. Then it all fell apart. But this time it was different. Before I was converted it was terrible when I hit the pits, but at least that was all I had to cope with; now I found myself with a new problem as well, a load of guilt for letting it all go. That was a really torturous time. Just then there was a change in the flat and another Christian girl moved in. Somehow Sue managed to pick me up a bit. She was great, actually choosing to join us in the flat just to help me. A number of the members of the church were helpful and understanding, but others, who were really ignorant about the problems of long-term addiction, thought that because I was now a Christian all my problems should have gone away. I wish! Two experienced counsellors realized my problem and felt that I should go to a women's Christian rehabilitation centre. Although I went for an interview, in the meantime I was sinking fast. Once again I found myself feeling suicidal, not wanting to live and not seeing a way out or any possibility of one.

A meeting with God

Late one night, after a whole day of drinking and drug abuse, I shut myself in my room with the television, radio and stereo all blaring to try to blank myself out from myself. Sue knew things were far wrong and she came in to check on me, then went into her own room. The only way I can describe what happened next is by saying that I had a real meeting with God. I could almost hear his voice. 'What are you doing? You gave your life to me and here you are with gritted teeth trying and trying and all you need to do is give your life to me. I can do it.' I thought I'd been at rock bottom before, but I'd never been anywhere like this. I was utterly broken. God didn't seem to be telling me off, he was gentle and loving and merciful. From the deepest darkness I reached up. 'Yea, I've had it,' I said, probably aloud. 'OK, God, over to you.' When I went in to tell Sue what had happened she was staggered I'd even been able to get up, I was in such a bad state. She was so pleased, especially as she was shortly to leave London and wanted to see me being cared for before she went.

Two days later I was in rehab, but not before I'd had a very profound experience. People from church came to be with me over that weekend and they prayed and prayed. If I woke up agitated, they prayed and I was given peace. As a result I went into rehab clean. Despite that good start, the eighteen months I was there was one of the hardest times of my life. It started with a strip search when I arrived and that was typical of the regime. We weren't allowed any money, couldn't go out on our own, our phone calls were listened to and our mail read. It felt brutal. However, as the months passed these privileges were given back to us as and when we were able to cope with them. I think it was particularly difficult for me because, despite all I'd done and gone through, I was actually a very proud and independent individual. There was a programme to be worked though, specific issues each week plus general counselling sessions. It could have been done in six months, but I knew that this had to be real for me. I had to do it thoroughly; there were deep things to be sorted out with God. These things were really important to me.

Quite a struggle

A couple of times during the year and a half there I came close to leaving but, because they wouldn't give us money, I would have had to run away. Some did that. I got through these times and struggled on though my nature made it quite a struggle. I remember after a session on the subject of failure, I wouldn't try anything in case I failed. I just couldn't grasp what was being explained to me. It took about ten further attempts at the session till the penny dropped. Now failure is not an issue with me. I feel comfortable about trying things if I think God wants me to do them, even if I'm not sure if I can do them. What was a terrible struggle for me in rehab is a real help to me now.

One aspect of my old lifestyle became a big problem during that long period of rehab. Some years before I had been involved in a serious road accident, so bad that it surprised the emergency services that I got out of it alive. The drugs I was taking at the time masked the pain, but when I was clean it hit me hard. For a while I was in hospital unable to walk. I didn't handle that well and felt very angry about it. One day, when I was lying in hospital, God spoke to my heart, telling me that even if I never moved again he couldn't love me more than he loved me then. That really broke through something inside me. From being angry I found myself lying worshipping God. It wasn't all wonderful after that, but the experience stayed with me and helped a lot, especially over the time I was in a body cast.

From rehab I went to live with a Christian family. In many ways that was wonderful but it was difficult too because it made me grieve for what I'd not known as a child. My experience in that home had an effect that has lasted until today, but it was often touch and go at the time. Then it was on to independent living again. I'd be lying if I gave the impression that everything went well. I really struggled, and a few times during the first year I went on drinking and using benders. They were worse than before I was a Christian because I felt so intolerably guilty. Other people felt let down when that happened, but nothing they said could make me feel worse than I did. Sometimes, just sometimes, over the years since then I've yearned for a drink and occasionally that has made me angry with God. He dealt with the drugs, taking away all desire to use them, why couldn't he do the same with drink? Yet I suppose I've learned a lot by being left with that occasional longing. If that had been taken away from me I might have had quite unrealistic expectations of others who were trying to quit their addiction. Because my experience has taught me not to judge others, people have told me they feel safe with me. I'm grateful for that because I know how much safe people meant to me.

An open door

As my back was still a problem, when I left rehab I couldn't work. That wasn't easy but it did open the door to do some studying. I did a one-year access course and followed that with a degree in psychology. It didn't really help me on a personal level but it has been a great help in the work I've done since then. We covered subjects like anorexia and bereavement and I also did child and adolescent psychology. Although my university friends were not Christians they were good to me. When drink was a potential problem they would suggest doing something by way of distraction. One or two of my student friends became Christians, which really thrilled me and gave the angels in heaven a thrill too. While I was at university I came into a new understanding of my relationship with God, seeing him as a heavenly dad, interested in the course I was doing and healing my hurts as I did it. But things were not plain sailing on the church front and the Lord led me to move to a congregation where I could have a fresh start and be known for who I was rather than what I had been. The people in my new congregation put their trust in me, which was just what I needed. Before long I was asked to teach in Sunday School and that was brilliant. I had reached a stage of needing to give out, of needing to tell what I had come to know for myself.

From university I went on to a Christian college. That was a warm time, not without its tough patches but very special despite them. Since my conversion I had a desire to study the Bible in depth because I was so aware of my ignorance of it and I also wanted training in evangelism as God seemed to be putting that on my heart. And at the end of my studies at Bible college I felt a real satisfaction of completing the course. I'd never totally finished anything before I was a Christian, now I'd completed rehab, my degree and a Bible college course as well. That meant a lot to me. Near the end of my course people started to mention London City Mission and I was put on a placement with them in London's East End. People told me I should think about working for LCM, and that's how I came to do what I'm doing now.

Power and love

My work with the Mission means I'm involved with all kinds of people. I don't meet my own past problems in them, though just very occasionally things are said and there is still a slight twinge, but that's not a bad thing, just a reminder. What helps me most from my previous experience is that I know through and through that the power and love of God can turn a life completely around. If he can do it for me he can do it for anybody because I've been through the lowest of the low. Because of my past, and because of what the Bible teaches, I don't judge. Who am I to do that? Instead, what I see around me makes me long to reach out and bring healing and the love of Christ to the most awful situations. Whether I see results or not, I'm content to reach out to the people God puts in front of me.

Sometimes I really feel the hurt of the pain I see around me. And sometimes the injustices I see make me angry. The Bible is not just about saving souls; it is also about justice. That disturbs me but it motivates me too. Christians should be bringing justice into society. They should be speaking out. So many believers have lost touch with the non-Christian world, and the

world is non-Christian and an unjust place.
It's when you sit around a table with people,
or on the wall outside a school, or on the
pavement when you're being real with folk
that you see it. The injustice of situations
stares you in the face and you have to do
something about it. You can't just sit and
let things happen. What I've discovered is
that the important thing is my relationship
with Jesus and that's what gets things done.
The more I focus on him, the more I look
around and the more I look forward. And
one day I know I'll see him face to face. That
means so much to me. I just long for that
day of fulfilment, every single day I long
for it.

I can't finish my story by giving the
impression that things always go brilliantly
now. There are still occasional down days,
days when the demon of suicide comes into
my mind. That's the devil's work and I know
it. But I choose life. Over and over and
over again I choose life. One day I'll see
Jesus face to face and that really will be life
and too wonderful for words.

Nine >> Tony Keating

I come from Liverpool and have no Christian background. Mum was against religion of any kind though she would have said she was Protestant. Dad was Catholic. They weren't happily married, and divorced when I was still quite young. After their divorce I became very anti-religion too. There was a lot of religion about Liverpool; it was quite a sectarian place. However, I rebelled against the idea of religion at all and became very anti Christian.

When I was fifteen years old I left school. The following year I married Chris and before I was twenty we had two children. By then it was the early seventies. There was no work in Liverpool at that time for the likes of me. Unemployment was high, employers could pick and choose who they wanted and I didn't present myself very well because I was a bit of a hippie.

Signed on

One day I told my wife I was going out to try to get a job on the buses. Because at the bus depot they didn't want to know me, I was too much of a hippie for their liking, I kept walking towards the centre of Liverpool. After a couple of miles I stopped in front of the Army Recruiting Office and looked in the window at a display showing guys on golden sand. A man appeared at my side – he was an Army sergeant. 'Do you want to look like that, son?' he asked. I looked at the sand and I thought of Liverpool. 'Yea,' I said, 'I do.' 'Come on in,' the sergeant invited. I went in the door and before I walked out again I had signed on as a soldier, a Guardsman. Me! 'Well, did you get a job on the buses?' Chris asked, when I got back home. 'No, I didn't,' I told her. And before she could say anything else, I went on, 'I'm in the Army.' She nearly fell over. Hippies didn't join the Army! But I had. Then came the hair-cut, and what a hair cut! I felt as though I'd been scalped!

It didn't take long for me to realize that I wasn't going to enjoy being in the Army. If I'd thought about it at all, I'd have known that before I signed up. For the next seven years I did all the public duties, serving at

Buckingham Palace, St Jame's Palace and all the rest. Some people are improved by an Army career; I was not. After seven years I was expert at three things: drinking, violence and racism. That's what I learned as a Guardsman. I should have known better than take to drink because my father died through drink when he was in his forties. Despite that, by the time I was in my mid-twenties I was well along the same road. And being a racist was almost part and parcel of being a Guard. There were no black people in the Guards and we were proud of that. It pains me to think what I was like then.

Where do I go from here?
When I came out of the Army I didn't know what to do with myself. Then I thought about the Prison Service and it seemed a logical choice. After all, it wasn't all that different from being a soldier, or so I thought. The job suited me fine. It paid enough money to keep the family and left plenty over for drink. Not only that, I could have as much violence as I liked. If there was a fight in the prison I was right in there with my fists and enjoyed it. I had a real macho image, and for me image was

everything. I knew what I wanted my reputation to be and made sure I lived up to it. In Bedford Prison I was one of the hard men, harder than many of the inmates. That's how it was for seven or eight years.

I began then to feel that there was something missing in my life though I had no idea what it was. We had enough money to do all we wanted, I earned well and my wife was working too. Yet there was still something missing. So I drank more, but for the first time in my life that didn't help. One night I was on duty with another gatekeeper, a man called Bob. We knew each other well; he was a nice man, even a good man. I asked Bob what the tie was that he was wearing. 'That means I'm a Christian,' he said. I recoiled. 'Keep that to yourself,' I warned him, and at the end of my shift I headed for the pub. These five words, 'That means I'm a Christian,' really bugged me. From then on I watched Bob like a hawk. He had a lovely way of calming both prisoners and staff; where there was discord he brought peace. Because he was an elderly man and not very fit I thought he shouldn't be in the job, but even I had to admit that he was able to do things that younger fitter men couldn't do. Although the last thing I wanted to think about was Christianity I couldn't help wondering if how Bob lived and worked had something to do with him being a Christian. I reckoned that it must be important to him if he wore a tie advertising what he believed.

Challenged

One day my daughter came home with a Gideon New Testament she had been given at school. 'Look at this, Dad,' she said. 'Take that upstairs!' I spat out. 'And don't let me see it again!' But one day when she wasn't at home I passed her open bedroom door and saw the New Testament lying on her bedside table. Picking it up, I stuffed it in my pocket and took it to work with me. Most lunchtimes I went out for a drink to fire me up for whatever trouble I would meet later – most fights were in the afternoon – but that day I walked to the River Ouse and started to read the New Testament. What a boring start, nothing but a list of begats! But I read on as far as Matthew chapter five where I reached the Beatitudes. Despite myself I was challenged. 'Blessed are the peacemakers,' it said. Never! I thought; it's the strong that survive. Then I remembered Bob. The list of people who were 'blessed' hit me because I was just the opposite of every one of them. Yet I had to admit that they described Bob well.

For weeks, maybe it was even months, I went down to the same place every lunchtime, and sat there trying to work out how anyone could be the kind of person Jesus described in the Sermon on the Mount. That's the name of the part of the Bible I was reading, and I was never able to get beyond it to anything else. I felt there was a greater force than I knew, that God did exist. Yet I knew that if there was a God I certainly wasn't acceptable to him because of the kind of person I was. I was a drunk. I was violent. And I was a racist. But as I was desperate I decided to God-shop, to go round the churches to see what they were peddling. I reckoned that you didn't buy anything without looking at it first, and I wasn't buying into religion without knowing what it was about. Soon I discovered that the local churches didn't have much of a sales pitch. Most of them were closed at lunchtime when I had time to go. Nobody knew what I was doing, certainly not Chris.

Searching for answers

In one church I went to there was a lady cleaning the place. When she told me that the vicar wasn't there I asked her if she could explain things to me. She pointed down the church and told me I could pray down there, but I didn't know how. Then I went to a Christian Science Reading Room where I met another lady. I asked her if she could help me understand what I was reading. She said she could help me, and handed me a book to read. But I told her I had enough trouble understanding the book I already had without starting on another one. Then I remembered another church; my wife and I had gone to it once when we first moved to Bedford. But there was singing and dancing and tamborines and we thought the people were off the wall, though they were friendly enough. That was our first and last visit there. Now I decided to go back. However, on the Saturday night I got as drunk as I had ever been in my life. For some reason I felt this was the last time I'd get drunk and I was going to make the most of it. 'Where are you going?' Chris asked the next morning when I got up and dressed. When I told her I was going to church she said I was still drunk and told me to go back to bed.

When I found the church we'd once gone to I discovered it had closed down. I went to the shop next door and asked what had happened. 'They've built a big place round the corner,' I was told. Round I went, but by the time I arrived the service had already started and the lady at the door took me right down to the front. There were about 300 people there, and they were all behind me. To my utter amazement I felt I had come home even though I thought they were a bit crazy with their singing and dancing and strange tongues and things. Then a man got up to speak. As he was very relaxed about it I asked what he meant when he said something I didn't understand. 'You keep quiet till I finish and I'll explain it to you,' he told me.

Close encounter

After the service the preacher asked how he could help me. I told him a bit about myself then showed him the Beatitudes in my daughter's New Testament. 'This really bugs me,' I said. 'I know a guy who's like this but I can't be accepted by God because my life stinks.' 'That's quite right,' the preacher said. I shrugged my shoulders. 'Thanks pal,' I grunted. 'That's all I need.'

Then he went on, 'It's like a New Year's resolution. You can't keep it up yourself. But if you admit to God that you're a sinner (that means that you're all wrong), and if you tell God that your life is in pieces, God will forgive you because Christ went to the cross for you. And when you have a relationship with God, the great news is that the Holy Spirit will help you to live the life you've read about because the Sermon on the Mount is a rule-book for Christians not for non-Christians'. There and then I prayed and the Holy Spirit entered my life.

'Where have you been?' Chris asked, when I got home. I told her I was a Christian. 'It'll not last past Monday,' she said, knowing how impulsive I am, yet remembering that even though she was a lapsed Catholic she had prayed for me for years. But it did last and I had a real zeal to see her saved too. I hassled her to come to church, telling her that the church I'd been to was the one we'd visited years before. Eventually one day she came and found it was just as it had been, only bigger. She found the whole thing offensive. Because I was so bothered I went to see the pastor. 'I love it here,' I told him, 'but I want to see my wife saved.' After he advised me to find somewhere she'd feel more comfortable, I went shopping again, to high churches and low churches, to middle churches and right out there on the edge churches. Either I found them full of people who didn't seem to believe the Bible, or I didn't like them or Chris didn't feel comfortable. It was a difficult time. 'Take me to that church,' she said one day, pointing to one we passed on the way to the shops. It was a Pentecostal church, and I knew the pastor, a West Indian, because he visited in the prisons. In fact, he'd invited me to church. The first church we went to was nothing compared to this and I thought Chris would just walk out. As a result I wasn't surprised when she got up and pushed past me, but I was when she went out to the front and was saved there and then. We became members of that church, the only whites in a congregation of two hundred black people.

Rejected

Some time later God gave me courage to visit the prison with the pastor. That was a real turn up for the books as I'd not told people I was a Christian. I went in wearing a suit and carrying a big Bible, inviting the inmates to a Bible study. My mates and the prisoners didn't cope. They looked away and were embarrassed for me, even the ones I thought were my friends. Although I felt rejected and upset, I had to come out. Before long people recognized I was different, they knew why, and they knew which church we were going to. Cartoons started to appear in the prison. One showed me in a big cooking pot with church members dressed in tribal costume dancing all around me. Things like that hurt me badly, and I lost friends too. There were times when I wondered if it was worth it. Before communion in our church we fasted for forty-eight hours and we also washed each other's feet because Jesus washed his disciples' feet in the Bible. As I knelt and washed an old man's gnarled feet he smiled down at me and I wept with joy because I knew God had taken the evil of racism away from me. Later that night I put my hand in my pocket for a cigarette, then realized I didn't want it. Racism and the desire for cigarettes were taken away in just one night.

God had to deal with my violence too. I knew that had to go, and it did. Eventually the Lord led me to apply for a nursing course in the prison. When I'd finished it, I went back to the same prison as a nurse.

Sometimes I could hardly believe I was me, and the inmates who had known me before I became a Christian had a problem believing it too. After a time the prison doctor asked me to help her open a unit for those who weren't coping with prison life. I was the butt of the staff's humour when I had cells painted in calming colours to help the prisoners relax! Because the unit worked so well the doctor asked me to go with her to London to open a similar one in a prison there. From a nice house in Bedford we moved to a grotty place in the East End of London next to a factory that gave off a terrible smell. It was the last place I wanted to go, but God seemed to be telling us both to go there. It's a long story, but it ended up that the doctor didn't come and the unit was never opened. But by then we had moved. Chris and our daughter found good jobs and I worked as a prison nurse, but I wasn't satisfied with what I was doing.

Challenged
We settled in an East End congregation and I helped the pastor to plant a new church. People kept asking why I didn't go into full-time ministry, and sometimes that bugged me. The hurdle was that we were so

comfortable in material things that it was hard to change. Then one day on my way to work I developed a terrible pain in my back, so bad I had to be carried home. After six months flat on my back I was retired on medical grounds. I was just in my early forties. At the time a London City Missionary was working in our small new congregation. 'Ever thought of working with the Mission?' he asked. I thought LCM was an old fashioned lot but I didn't say so. 'I don't think that's for me,' I replied. But he was persistent, taking me to see some of the work of the Mission. Almost despite myself I applied and got through the selection system. Now I run a Christian Centre in an area that is over 90 per cent Asian, and most of my congregation of forty are Afro-Carribean. Within eight hundred yards of the Centre there are seven mosques and there's a Sikh temple next door. I often think that I wouldn't like to meet the man I was when I was a racist.

It is the biggest privilege of my life to minister to the people in the area, the very kind of people I once hated, I once cursed in my drunken rages. Chris helps me in the work. She keeps the books, teaches Sunday School and does other things too.

Without her I couldn't do what I do, and without the grace of God neither of us would want to do it at all.

Ten >> Bob Stanton

My first appointment as a London City Missionary was at the Turkey Street Mission in Enfield. At my welcome service I was told, 'You'll find it a heartbreak corner around here.' I thought, 'Thanks for the welcome.' The Mission was right opposite a pub called The Plough Inn. I quite often thought about the name of the pub. I felt I was ploughing in the area, breaking up the hard ground and sowing the seed of the Word of God. We had activities during the week for children and young people, and a Sunday School and evening service each Sunday. My wife, Margaret, led a weekday meeting for women and we also started a men's meeting. As I visited door-to-door I invited people to our meetings and services. I felt as though I had two congregations: the one that came to worship on Sundays and the one I visited during the week.

An elderly lady who used to come to the Centre on Sundays and to women's meetings during the week found it increasingly difficult as the years went on. By the time she was 89, she was unable to come at all. I decided to visit her each week and I used to go on a Thursday afternoon. One day I had to rearrange my schedule because of a deputation meeting and I decided to go in the morning instead. The Lord's hand was in that change of plan. I rang her doorbell and waited, knowing it would take time for her to get to the door with her zimmer frame. When she didn't come, I rang the bell again and waited still further. There was no response to the second ring either. Because I was anxious for her I looked through the letterbox and, when I did so, I saw smoke in the hallway and smelled burning. I ran to the phone box and dialled 999. The fire brigade, which was there in a short while, found the lady in the back room of her bungalow. She had fallen and knocked over the electric fire that was lying, face down, on the carpet in a smoke-filled room. Although her hair and her clothing were singed, she was not burnt. I praised God for that. The lady was taken to hospital suffering from shock. A little while later a reporter from the local paper came to see me asking for details for a story. At the end of our conversation the reporter said, 'It's not every day you're involved in saving people.' 'I know what you mean,' I replied, 'but that's what it's all about.' On that occasion it was a lady's life that was saved, but it has also been my privilege over the years to see souls saved by God's grace.

Eyes up

One Sunday evening a young housewife arrived at the Centre and she came to know the Lord that night. Previously she used to spend a lot of her time at the bingo hall and she continued to go for a short time after her conversion. One evening, not long afterwards, she was at the bingo hall when she wondered if the Lord wanted her to be there and to be gambling. She said afterwards that she realized that instead of having her eyes down on the card, she should have her eyes up to the Lord. The young woman grew in grace and in the knowledge of the Lord Jesus Christ and she became a great help to us and a real witness to her family. She moved away from our district but she did not move away from the Lord whom she continues to serve to this day.

Wherever we have lived in our service to the Lord, we have tried to have a concern for our immediate neighbours. In Ealing the missionaries who were there before us had shared the same concern. Well before my time there was a large family living next door but one to the Mission and the mother used to send all the children to Sunday School. In the Lord's providence one of the younger members of that family, long since moved from the area, came back and was a great source of joy to us. Scripture tells us that one sows and another reaps and that certainly was the case with Mavis. The sowing was done many years before we met her, and the reaping also, yet the Lord graciously allowed us to see part of a further harvest.

Jack and Mavis Elmer

Jack

I was brought up in a poor home in West London. My father was out of work nine months of the year and my mother, who was a wonderful woman, worked her fingers to the bone. She took in washing and ironing to keep food on the table and clothes on our backs. I remember when the rent man came knocking at the door we had to be quiet in order that he would think there was noone in. It wasn't such a bad life for kids but it must have been hard on our parents. We were always scrounging, even sometimes pinching things off the counters in Woolworths. That was the only way we ever got a treat. I wasn't a rogue, but I certainly wasn't an angel. Everybody round about was in the same boat as ourselves and we all looked after each other. That kind of help is really lacking now.

At the end of my years at an elementary school I failed my Eleven Plus exam. My headmaster must have thought I should have passed because I remember him being surprised that I didn't. Failing the exam didn't bother me and I enjoyed the secondary school I went to. The Second World War was still being fought when I left school and I found a job in a factory making Mosquito aeroplanes. I worked the sawing and planing machines, which was really quite interesting. That was my first experience of working life and I liked it.

Years later, when I was working as a fitter with North Thames Gas Board, I met Mavis. She was a clerk in the office and every day I had to go in to see her. Mavis used to say that I always smelled of TCP, but at least that gave us something to talk about! Although she was fourteen years younger than me that didn't stop us becoming friends, and the fact that Mavis was a Christian set me thinking. My parents were not churchgoers but as a child I had been sent to Sunday School twice every Sunday. I'd never doubted that God existed, but Christianity made no impression on me whatever, at least until I got to know Mavis.

Bamboozled!
My friend had attended the London City Mission since childhood and her faith meant a lot to her. Mavis loved reading her Bible and was involved in the work of the Christian Centre. One Sunday evening she took me to the service there. I enjoyed the singing and the preaching was interesting but I was really put off at the end. A man came up to me and bamboozled me with religious dogma in quite an aggressive way. As we left I told Mavis that I would never go back again; it was too foreign to me. It was many years before I did go back and then things were very different for I really enjoyed it. And when the missionary, Mr Bob Stanton, preached the gospel, it spoke

right to my heart. He had an amazing way of applying the Bible to our everyday lives. It was not long before I felt that it was a wasted Sunday if Mavis and I didn't go to the service together.

I became involved in the Mission's work myself and spent a fair bit of time with Mr Stanton. I helped him with little jobs around the place and I also went to the men's meeting where the fact that I shone at darts made me quite popular! There were games to start with at the meeting then a short service afterwards. Mr Stanton tied in what he said there to the Sunday message and I learned a lot. Then there was the prayer meeting one evening to which Mavis and I also went. Our time revolved round the Mission, and that made a wonderful life for us. But there was even better to come. One Sunday evening, in a normal evening service, it was as though I left this poor world behind. Mr Stanton invited people out to the front to state their love of the Lord. Even if I had wanted to, I couldn't have stopped myself. I just had to go out. I broke down with emotion at the thought of all Jesus had done for me on the cross. That evening changed my life.

I've never lost my love for the Lord

though I have had times when I've struggled. Most of my struggles have been against my own inadequacy. Whatever I do for the Lord it can never equal what he has done for me. But that's the wonder of the gospel, that Jesus did it all on the cross and that I can do nothing whatever to save myself. It's a strange thing that it's the wonderful freeness of God's salvation that I sometimes find hard to accept. I keep wanting to try to repay him, even though I know I will never be able to do that. I'm not able to get out now much because walking is a problem due to a heart condition, but day by day I try to achieve a closer walk with the Lord. My Bible is always beside me and my times of prayer are precious to me.

Often I find myself thinking about heaven, of the joyful existence we'll have in the presence of the Lord. There will be no more pain there and no ill health. I long to be free of that, though it saddens me to think of Mavis being left alone. The fourteen years difference in our ages didn't seem very much when we were young but it seems a lot now. Yet Mavis is strong in the Lord and he'll look after her when I'm no longer here.

Mavis

I come from a large family of seven boys and six girls. I was number twelve of the thirteen. Among my earliest memories are seeing Mum opening letters and crying as she read them. They were from my older brothers who were fighting in the war. I was five when the last baby in the family was born and I felt very pushed out. I think the people at the Mission we went to realized that and were especially good to me. I received a lot of love and kindness there and I loved going. When I was a little girl it was the companionship that meant most to me, but that changed when I was eleven for that's when I became a Christian. I thank God for the London City Mission, because it was through the Mission that I came to know the Lord Jesus.

The missionary then, Mr Tom Gray, had children about my own age and I felt almost part of his family. He nurtured me like a father. As I grew up Mr Gray encouraged me to apply for nursing training at Mildmay Missionary Hospital. I really wanted to do that. Sadly, my father had just died and Mum decided that I should stay at home and get a job. She issued me an ultimatum, saying that if I left to go nursing there wouldn't be a bed for me when I came back. At the time that was hard, but looking back I realize that if I'd gone into nursing I'd never have met Jack.

Fire!

My first job was with Scripture Gift Mission (SGM), and while working there the Lord spared my life in an amazing way. I was working in the showroom, which was in and under an office with a glass front. There was a gas leak in the basement and a gasman passed me on his way down to work on it. Suddenly there was a huge explosion – the gas main had ignited and set the building on fire. The engineer was injured and a lady who was in the showroom speaking to a Maltese gentleman from the BBC was badly injured. The poor man was killed. The glass frontage of the offices fell in front of me and protected me. I walked out of the rubble unhurt, although the building was completely destroyed. London City Mission Headquarters were just across the road from were I was working and someone there lent me a coat and gave me money to get home. My coat and other personal things were lost in the fire, including a Bible I'd been given by SGM when I answered five hundred questions in writing. I did that course through my local London City Mission where I received a great deal of encouragement. SGM was kind enough to give me another Bible to replace the one that was lost. I had a bad time of feeling down in the dumps after that. It was probably a reaction to Dad's death, not being allowed to nurse and the explosion. Despite all these things God was very real to me then and I knew he was looking after me.

I was working in an office when I first met Jack. As he always wore such lovely white shirts I assumed he was married and thought he probably had children too; It was a nice surprise to discover that he was single. Because I was a Christian I wanted Jack to be one too, which was why I took him along to the Mission. Unfortunately what began as a good evening ended disastrously when a very zealous man collared Jack and started preaching at him. That could have turned my friend off for life; it did for many years. And, sadly, I have to confess that my attendance lapsed too.

Steering clear of Sunday
Over that time a lady from the Mission always remembered to send me birthday

and Christmas cards but, although we only lived a few miles away, I never made any effort to see her. One year I sent her a Christmas card and wrote on it that we should get together one day. She phoned me about Easter time the following year and asked us for tea. We went, but we steered clear of a Sunday. Her husband was out at the men's meeting at the Mission and when he came in he enthused to Jack about it. I felt so embarrassed, but my husband wasn't at all put out. Jack went with him the following week and before long we were there every Sunday. Although I'd been away for a long time we were greeted as friends. That meant a lot to me. We were soon there every week and one wonderful Sunday evening Jack became a Christian.

Bob Stanton, missionary

In 1983, Mavis gave her testimony at a women's meeting anniversary. She had just recommenced coming to the Mission after twenty years. We praised the Lord that this backslider had been restored. As my wife and I visited Mavis and her husband it was a joy to speak to them both about the things of God. When Jack requested that I explain to him how to become a Christian it was a joy to point him to the Lord. I remember the evening service when he came forward in response to an appeal. He told me that he had asked the Lord into his life and stated that he was really enjoying the nearness of the Lord Jesus. How we praised the Lord for this.

It was a joy to us to watch Jack and Mavis continue with the Lord and to see how open they were to God's Word as preached in our services. Following our Easter service the year after Jack came to the Lord, he wrote to me in these terms, 'I feel I should let you know the blessing your Easter services were to me; the grim reality of the crucifixion, then the joy of the resurrection... I thank God for the opportunity to have friendship and worship at the Mission. I know it is all the Lord's work but in my heart I couldn't let Easter pass without thanking you for all your time and effort.' My response to Jack's moving letter was to acknowledge that it was all by God's grace and all for his glory.

A little over two years later Jack, seriously ill as a result of a heart attack, was to go into hospital for heart surgery. This was the second time in five years he had needed heart surgery and on this occasion he was to have a triple bypass. We were praying very much for him and his wife at this time of crisis and we praised the Lord that they felt helped and blessed by God. We especially praised him because Jack was going on with the Lord day by day despite the trying time he was going through. I distinctly remember I had planned in my preaching to go through the book of James, and the subject for the evening before Jack was to go into hospital was how to face trials. Even as late as the Sunday afternoon I was thinking that I could not preach that sermon with Jack facing surgery. I was to have said that we had to count it all joy to face trials, but I was greatly exercised over it. Yet I felt the Lord wanted me to continue as I had planned. The sermon I preached had four points: that we face trials with joy because we have Jesus with us; that God has a purpose in every trial; that there is a reward promised to all who undergo trials; and that we should face trials with single-minded devotion to the Lord. Afterwards I was reassured that the Word had been blessed to Jack and Mavis.

The Elmers now live on the South Coast where they recently celebrated their fortieth wedding anniversary. Jack, who is in poor health and becoming increasingly weak, can have no further surgery. Yet in all the trials that beset them, Jack and Mavis are looking to the Lord and trusting in him.

Eleven >> Adam Davidson

Although I live and work in London, I'm from the Lake District. I was born there in 1975. When I was two years old, my two sisters and I were taken into care. For a while we went from foster home to foster home, seven of them in two years, never being left anywhere long enough to settle down. The main problem was that there were three of us, and although foster parents have big hearts not many have big enough hearts or homes to take in three children. Then it seemed things turned a corner for us. We were placed in a good home with a happy family. That was an amazing experience after all we had been through and we really began to feel at home. The family lived on a farm. There was space to play, plenty of scope for three extra children and the security of a family atmosphere. There was even a horse! It was like something from an Enid Blyton story book. But tragically the daughter of the family took ill and died. Her parents couldn't cope with their grief and with the three of us. We were moved out and on. I was four years old.

My sisters and I were put into emergency care for the weekend with a widow whose family had grown up. Her name was Marion, and she turned out to be a real blessing to us. She understood us and recognized our need to be together and to stay together. Marion knew that the more often we were shunted on the less likely we were to be placed as a family unit. When she heard that we were actually to be separated on leaving her, she dug in her heels and what was intended to be a weekend in her care eventually extended to several years.

Marion also lived in the country and she had goats, dogs, cats, rabbits and guinea pigs. It was just what we needed. Although her home was comfortable, she wasn't wealthy. But with Marion my sisters and I lacked for nothing, especially love. Our new foster mother had love in abundance. She wasn't just there to look after us, in a very deep way she was there for us. We could trust her, we could rely on her and we knew we were loved. Home life was good with Marion, and it was fun too. A rally track ran round the back of her house and I loved, just loved, going out there when the cars came whizzing past. Marion didn't particularly like it but we certainly did.

The village school

My first school was in a small village in the Lake District. We liked it there and were happy. Mum (we soon called Marion Mum) was a very hands-on carer, even when it came to school. As one of my sisters had suffered from a very cranky teacher Mum refused to let me go into her class. All major decisions had to be formalized with the social services, but Mum didn't hesitate to do that, and she had us moved to a two teacher school she thought would be better for us. It was. There were just two pupils in my 'class' and seven in the year below me. I think there must have been a baby boom that year! I knew every pupil well in the two roomed school and I really loved being there. The teachers were devoted to what they were doing. School seemed to be their life. As the headmaster kept a garden in the grounds of the school we learned practical things there too. It wasn't just all about books. I discovered then that there is more to education than what can be learned from school books. Because my sisters and I had been moved around so much the closeness of this little school did us good.

The atmosphere there was not at all pressured and simple things helped to heal the hurts of our young lives. For example, the children all came from local farms and their parents knew each other and saw each other regularly. We were absorbed into the community as well as the school. And, as time passed, we began to relax in the security of Marion's home and the little school. But through no fault of Mum's or ours that was to change. She became ill, and because she was a widow and there was nobody else in the house to care for us, we were removed to a children's home some distance away. Nowhere could be found locally that could take all three of us.

A nightmare begins

The home was an old building, a great big place. We were taken there late at night and dumped with all our stuff in what seemed to be a huge hall. It was like something out of *Oliver Twist*. I was upset, confused and utterly miserable. Marion wasn't there and I knew she was ill. Everything was strange and we were exhausted and frightened. My sisters were shown where they were to sleep and I was taken to a big room with several beds in it and told which was mine. I rushed to the window feeling that I needed to be able to look out. I was eight at the time, just a little boy. I was told when breakfast was and that we would be going to school the next day. No thought was given to comforting us or explaining things to us or to making us feel at home. It was as though we had been deserted. The social worker that dealt with us was horrible, and that's not just a matter of a small boy's opinion.

Things didn't get any better. I wanted to be back in the country, the home was in a town. I needed space to get away from other people but there was no place to go. From being just the three of us at home with Marion, we were shoved into a big home along with some children who were quite seriously disturbed. Instead of eating Mum's cooking at the kitchen table, we were forced to eat at a huge table with the others. And one thing especially was awful for all three of us; we were expected to call the staff members 'auntie' and 'uncle'. That may seem a small thing or even a good idea, but for children whose family life has been so fractured to have the pretence of family imposed by strangers, and not always very nice ones, it was hideous and just added to our misery.

As the rule in the home was that we went to bed at our age, I went at eight o'clock. Another boy, he was about fifteen years old, came to my bed and said he would read me a story. By then I was starved of the affection Marion had given me, and the boy's kindness was welcome. He seemed gentle and I appreciated that. But what seemed innocent friendship turned out to be the opposite. The boy was homosexual and his behaviour towards me was wrong. Like most abused children, before I even began to realize the inappropriateness of what was happening I was caught in a web and unable to escape. He held me to ransom in the way that abusers do.

Nobody who has not experienced a children's home like that one can understand what I went through. Despite what that boy did he still seemed kinder than many of the others. For example, there was a lad there because he had smashed a bottle in his mother's face. Because he was too young for prison he was sent to the home instead. Another older boy enjoyed getting the younger ones into all kinds of trouble. Windows were broken and other destructive things done. That sort of thing had a kind of thrill to it but we got into terrible bother, and of course it was always the youngest ones who were caught. Some of the children had special educational needs and attended a school nearby. There was no stability as there were always children arriving and others leaving. On one occasion a family of six children arrived and had to be absorbed. I knew what they felt like. Looking back on it, there seemed to be a core of 'rejects' and the rest came and went. Within that group of displaced and disturbed children my abuser sometimes seemed better than many of the others.

There was one member of staff who was different, and I didn't mind calling him 'uncle'. Looking back I know he was a Christian. His face radiated the love of Jesus and he helped me a lot. Sadly my most distressing memory of my time in that shameful home is to do with that good man. When he was putting me to bed one night he bent down to give me a fatherly and totally innocent kiss, but abuse had wounded me and I pushed him away. Because he was a man I didn't trust him. It pains me to think about it even now. I was a little boy desperate for love and affection and I couldn't accept it when it was offered. Not only that, but I couldn't explain to him what had frightened me, probably because he was a man.

My punishment

My sisters and I thought we were in that place for ever and that was very scary. The abuse continued until one of the night staff realized that the boy regularly came into my room when I was going to bed. Then it all turned into my fault. I was asked why I hadn't told anyone, why I hadn't run away? The house authority's way of not coping with it was to pass the blame on to me. I felt betrayed. I was betrayed. The boy was punished and told not to go to my room again. That was his punishment. My punishment was to go through many years of believing that I was guilty of what had happened, while I was too young even to understand it. My sisters knew nothing about it until many years later. I don't know why, but I needed them not to know. Our time there spoilt my relationship with them in other ways too. It was survival of the fittest. The three of us had our own ways of coping or not, and we never really functioned as a threesome again.

The Christmas we spent there was the worst one of my life. Kind people from near Marion's home and the pupils in the two teacher school sent us little presents and every single one had a label saying who had sent it. I put two and two together and concluded there was no Santa Claus. That was a terrible blow for a little boy in need of all the security he could get. The long-term residents got bikes and things from the Social Work Department. We were technically short-term. I got a box of dominoes. It is many years ago, but I remember waking up that morning with a feeling of anticipation and I remember it being shattered. I'd thought Christmas would have some magic even in the home, but it didn't. I've never really been able to celebrate Christmas since then; it has too many sad memories.

Home again ... but damaged

Eventually, after nearly a year, we were allowed to go back to Marion. My oldest sister was already there as she had become sixteen while she was in the home and was therefore able to leave. I went back to the small school, but nothing was ever the same again. I had built up a barrier that even Mum couldn't get through. And I didn't tell her or anyone else what had happened to me. The home had 'neglected' to record the incident. When we were taken away from Marion I had begun to come out of my shell, but by the time we went back to her I was very firmly back inside it. And I couldn't let anyone near enough to help, not even Mum, although I desperately wanted to. That was how it was until the night *Childline* was launched. Mum, who suspected something, asked me if anything had happened to me that I wanted to talk about. Somehow the fact that abuse was being discussed on television allowed me to blurt out the story. It was such a relief to tell her, though it didn't take away the pain or the hurt.

The message in the mirror

Two years after that Mum changed jobs and we went to live in a nearby town. There were only three of us by then as my oldest sister had moved away. I started my first year of secondary school not long afterwards and I went to the Christian Union. That was Mum's Christian influence. She had given us Bibles and we went to church with her. We weren't forced to go, we just did because she did. There was another Christian influence in my life, a boy at school whose faith just shone out of him. He seemed full of joy and peace. On 21 February 1990 I told him that I wanted whatever it was that he had. He told me to go and ask Mum about it. I rushed home from school and, sitting with Marion at the kitchen table, I asked the Lord to come into my life. One of my preoccupations up until that day was working out in graphic detail how I could take my own life. The next morning I went into the bathroom and looked in the mirror. For the first time I could look myself in the eye and say, 'You're actually all right really.' It sounds stupid, but I danced round the bathroom and I kept going back to the mirror to look at myself. From wanting to take my own life, I'd suddenly been given the gift of life. And I recognized something when I looked in the mirror that morning ... I saw that like my school friend I had peace and joy, especially peace. And I felt secure. I was nearly fifteen years old.

Although things in my past still angered and hurt me, I was different and I knew it. I decided that I'd check out the other church in the town, partly because I wanted to see which one I liked best, and partly (mostly?) because it was nearer home and I wanted to get back to see the Formula One racing on television. The minister and his wife welcomed me and the congregation did too. There were lovely godly men there who showed real Christian love to me, though I still had a problem trusting them. I started to learn about Christian behaviour and lifestyle though I carried a lot of baggage from my past. I wanted to learn, and Jesus said that those who seek would find. That was true for me.

Ground rules

One thing that really impressed me was that when the godly men in the congregation spoke about the Bible their faces lit up. They probably have no idea what their conversations meant to me or the lasting impression they would leave. Eventually I asked to join the church, a serious thing in my denomination, as I had to be interviewed by the elders and tell them how I came to faith. I'll never forget their radiance on that occasion; I can only describe the evening as joyous. My minister laid down ground rules for me, and I needed them. They included attending both Sunday services and the midweek meeting too. It was a struggle, but I'd become wild and he knew I needed the discipline. It did me good. Joining the church was an amazing thing because the two others who joined with me somehow became my family. They are still very precious to me. Whenever I go back there I'm welcomed as a member of their families. Perhaps only someone who comes from my sort of background can really begin to appreciate what that means. The congregation was ageing, but they were beautiful people. Although I was just a boy they took me seriously. They trusted me with membership, and with being part of the family of faith, with all the responsibilities that involved. Another lesson I learned from them is that God's love is part of that family life, and there is plenty of it to go round and to spare. I thank God for those early years that meant so much to me. It was the beginning of my healing.

Mum decided to give up her job and find somewhere else to live and I moved with her. It was a terrible wrench to leave the church and the people there, but we had to go. I think it was then that I started coping with adult life. Not long after I'd completed a computer course at a local college, Swiss friends of Mum's, whom we'd not seen for several years, came to visit. To my amazement Mum asked if I'd like to go to Switzerland. The idea of getting away for a month seemed really good and she managed to scrape together the money from somewhere. That time abroad gave me growing space. While I was there I went through the issues of my life, and faced up to the fact that I could either go on with the Lord or let what had happened in the past eat me up. In a very odd way I was afraid to let go of the hurt I had lived with for so long; yet a verse in the Bible about casting all our cares on Jesus because he cares for us kept coming into my mind. What happened over those weeks is deeply personal and not for sharing, but I did cast my cares on Jesus. And if I hadn't done, I couldn't do the work I do now with the London City Mission.

I've been there
There have been ups and downs, some of them big ones. Healing doesn't come in a

day or a year, and I don't think it will come fully until I'm home in heaven. There is no way I will say that God caused what happened to me as a boy, but I know for sure he can use it. When I meet someone who is suicidal I can empathize, and it's the same with those who have been abused or in care. I can listen without judging and I can say that I understand. I really do. And often I'm aware when I meet someone that they have a story similar to mine and I'm prepared to wait until they are able to tell it to me. That's God's gift of discernment. It is in ways like these that God redeems the things I went through as a child, by using them to lead me to him and to enable me to reach out to others with his love. I sometimes tell people that in my experience becoming a Christian was like letting God's love shine in one room of my life, the place where there was greatest need at the time. For me that was the need of peace, joy and security. Over the years he has moved from room to room, shedding light into the dark corners of rejection and despair, and all my other hurts, even shedding some light into the darkest corner of all, the abuse. And one day it will all be lit by his glory, and that day I'll be in heaven.

Twelve >> 'Loose Ends'

ight in the City has told the stories of some of the people whose lives have intersected in London, within the parts of the city where the London City Mission works. It is not the kind of book where everyone lives happily ever after. Life –and especially life in the inner city – is not like that. People are not like that, either. There are always loose ends. The book can serve as a series of case studies to help us study the city, and the ministry that is needed to reach the people of the city.

Light in the City is not a book where everyone becomes a sincere and stable Christian. Again, real life is not like that. Some of the people seem to have decisively rejected Christianity. Others seem to have a sizeable question mark hanging over their religious condition. But many of the stories share a common factor, in telling how a life has been drastically affected by a faith-commitment to Jesus Christ. Sometimes from the most appalling of situations, these people have re-invented themselves – or, rather, found their lives re-invented by something or someone for whom they had previously had no time or interest.

That is the final loose end for every reader. 'Where does my story fit in? Is Jesus Christ the answer, even to deep questions that I've not yet asked?' The Jesus spoken of throughout this book is the Jesus of the Bible, and can be read about and encountered in its pages, especially in the Gospels of Matthew, Mark, Luke and John. He can also be met in the worship, preaching and community of local churches. He is no further away than a prayer.

The London City Mission is a fellowship of evangelical Christians, working to take the good news about Jesus to the people of London who do not yet go to church. The Mission was founded in 1835, and has played a significant part in the social and spiritual story of the capital. Today, it is still at work in a growing range of ministries, and is always recruiting men and women to carry on the work of making Christ known through words and deeds.

For further information about the London
City Mission, write to the following address

London City Mission
175 Tower Bridge Road
LONDON
SE1 2AH

Tel: 020 7407 7585
Fax: 020 7403 6711

Or look at there website

www.lcm.org.uk

Christian Focus Publications publishes biblically accurate books for adults and children. The books in the adult range are published in three imprints.

Christian Heritage contains classic writings from the past.

Christian Focus contains popular works including biographies, commentaries, doctrine, and Christian living.

Mentor focuses on books written at a level suitable for Bible College and seminary students, pastors and others; the imprint includes commentaries, doctrinal studies, examination of current issues and church history.

For a free catalogue of all our titles, please write to:

Christian Focus Publications, Ltd
Geanies House, Fearn,
Ross-shire, IV20 1TW, U.K.

For details of our titles visit us on our website

http://www.christianfocus.com